Driving
Ms. Dottie

By Larry Ferguson

with Mike Collins

Woodland Gospel
PUBLISHING HOUSE
A Division Of Woodland Press, LLC

Published In Beautiful West Virginia by
WOODLAND GOSPEL PUBLISHING HOUSE
A DIVISION OF WOODLAND PRESS, LLC
www.woodlandgospel.com

SAN: 2 5 4 – 9 9 9 9

Foreword

I have always loved people, and many have been faithful to come hear me sing for years. However, because of the hurt I have suffered since the age of twelve, I have allowed only a few people into my heart. When I met Larry Ferguson, I somehow realized immediately I could trust him and allowed him access to my heart, ministry and life.

Several years ago, Larry found me in a coma one morning and eventually flat lining in his and my friend Kate Collier's presence. Little did I know I would suffer four more comas that same year. Later I would wake up on life support and I don't think you will have a hard time guessing whose face I saw first—my precious friend Larry Ferguson. I give God glory that Larry was the one that sought out and found doctors with the right tools to put my health back on the right path.

Larry is more than a manager for me; he is a dear friend. Through the years, I have found him to be an honest businessman, wonderful Christian, faithful husband and devoted father. I have said it time and again: Larry and Judy work with me, not for me.

I believe with all my heart Larry Ferguson is one of the best examples of a Christian I have ever witnessed. He is a joy to be with while traveling, and is one of the funniest, understanding, compassionate and honest people I have ever had the privilege to know.

In fact, I couldn't have handpicked a son that would have been as loving, devoted and loyal to me if I tried. Reba was the only child I had naturally, but I adopted Larry and his family (in my heart) a long time ago. I love him. I love Judy, Christian and Pierce, too.

After laughing and crying for years over things that have happened to us while on the road, we have often joked that these stories would make a great book. So when Larry told me he wanted to write it; I knew it would be something special! He'd never written a book before, so when he let me read a few excerpts, I was totally amazed! As you will soon see, he is a natural storyteller!

I am so proud of him I could just burst! I couldn't be more proud of him and the job he has done with this project. I am convinced God is rewarding him for the many years of service he has devoted to me and other artists.

Some of the stories you are about to read will make you laugh. Some will make you cry. But all will give you an insight to what it's like on the road taking the Gospel all over the world.

Hide and watch, the success of this book is going to be a big surprise to many people—*Larry Ferguson included!*

May God bless the hands that wrote this book. I know it will bless the many people who will read it. Larry and I feel honored that Mike Collins, Keith Davis and everyone at Woodland Press have welcomed us into their publishing family. I believe this clever and marvelous book will stand on its own as one of a kind. I leave my blessings and fingerprints all over this project. Larry, I love you very much!

Your other mother,

Dottie Rambo

Introduction

What can I say about Dottie Rambo that someone else hasn't already said? We know her as the Queen of Gospel music, Songwriter of the Century, First Lady of Christian music—the titles are endless. However, the Dottie Rambo *I* know is a well that runs much deeper than any of these titles can describe. The many awards, tributes and accomplishments barely touch the surface of this woman's gifts reflected in her prolific pen and caring heart.

Looking at her small frame, you can't help but stand amazed at her larger-than-life personality and huge God-given talent. Only a person chosen by God could have the influence Dottie has on the church world and American music history in general.

In a time when most legendary figures are winding down, Dottie Rambo has remained active both as a performer and composer. This is for a good reason: she is not just an artist or songwriter, but a modern-day prophet through song. With the movement of her pen, God sends us a message, giving the listener hope, peace, comfort and knowledge of a Biblical truth.

Many threads are in the quilt that makes Dottie Rambo who she is, and through this book, I hope to show you a lighter side of the woman who has blessed my life again and again.

I want to make this clear. This book is not a biography. Dottie will release her own life story in the future, as only she can tell it. This book is but a journal of fun and adventure while on the road playing sidekick to the songbird as she spreads her wings delivering her music all over the country. Some of my greatest laughs, heartaches and spiritual awakenings have taken place alongside this woman. Dottie has made an imprint on my heart that I will take to the grave.

—*Larry Ferguson*

Chapter 1
My Mamma Did Dance and My Daddy Did Rock and Roll

I'm amazed at how God works in our lives.

—Larry Ferguson

Some of you won't admit to knowing the song *Your Mama Don't Dance and Your Daddy Don't Rock-n-Roll,* but you've probably heard it. Well, my childhood memories were the exact opposite of that song. My mom *did* dance and my dad *did* rock-n-roll. I don't mean that with any disrespect or in a negative sense. My mom, Jackie, loved to dance (and I don't think dancing is a sin, although some would disagree) and my dad was a rock-n-roll musician with aspirations of the big-time.

Mom was a factory worker and to this day, I think she is the hardest working person I have ever known. My father, Larry (I'm his namesake), taught guitar and played in rock bands before going into business for himself at the House of Guitars in my hometown of Louisville, KY.

Music was a major part of my life. In fact, my earliest memories are of Dad playing guitar on the couch and our basement becoming a rehearsal hall for his bands. My father is one of the most talented musicians I have ever known. Although his main gift is guitar, if you name an instrument, he can usually play it. If he doesn't know how to play it, he can learn it in no time at all. Musical instruments and equipment always filled our house, and as a young child, I knew these instruments were special. I also knew it was my duty to guard them when other children came over to play.

Dad's record collection focused solely on rock music, and our car radio never left the rock channel. While most parents forbid their children to listen to rock-n-roll, my father made it clear I was to listen to nothing else. We had rules in our house, and rule number one was that no other form of music was to be played in our house or car. We could only listen to rock-n-roll. Mom didn't mind the rule and I was too young to care.

Before going any further, let me say that although Dad was a rock musician and had an iron grip on what we could listen to, he was extremely conservative. Both my parents were conservative in morals and values. Mom and Dad never indulged in alcohol or drugs and our home-life was structured and/or balanced morally...just not musically.

Larry, at four months old, with Dad

Being an only child in a home where both parents were always on the go or working, I had to find things to occupy my time. Dad's music room was often my unrestricted temptation. Knowing I was never to touch them, I would mischievously play with Dad's guitars, drums, and microphones. It was a musical playground and I knew from an early age I wanted to work in the music industry. I thought I was going to be a singing superstar. It wasn't until later that I realized you had to be able to *sing* to be a singing superstar—cut me some slack, I was just a kid.

My father was a Christian and attended a Baptist church, and Mom grew up in a devout Catholic family. After marrying, neither wanted to give up his or her own faith and practices, and being young and stubborn, chose not to go to church at all. Despite this, Mom instilled in me a strong belief in honoring our God, who was Jesus, and taught me to pray at an early age. Although I was too young to understand, the seed had found fertile soil.

Larry, age two, with Aunt Mildred

During the late 70's and

Dad, Mom and Larry

early 80's, pop music was taking over the rock airwaves and country singers were beginning to cross over into the pop and rock markets. Several country songs had leaked into the rock circuit and aired on Dad's favorite stations. One song in particular was Dolly Parton's *9 to 5*. I had no idea this song would introduce me to a world I had never dreamed existed.

Unlike most children, I spent most of the time alone or with adults. I preferred adult company because I didn't have childhood peers. I jumped at every opportunity to visit either of my grandmothers. On one particular visit with my Grandma Ferguson, I started singing the song *9 to 5* all through the house while my grandmother and Aunt Mildred laughed.

"So you like Dolly Parton, huh?" my Aunt Mildred asked.

"No," I said. "Who is she?"

Aunt Mildred smiled and said, "She's the one that sings the song you're singing."

As avid country music fans, both Aunt Mildred and Grandma Ferguson loved that I had found a country song I liked. They loved this because they hated all rock-n-roll music—*except Elvis Presley, of course.*

"Would you like to see the movie *9 to 5* since you like the song so much?" Aunt Mildred asked.

"Yes!" I screamed. There was nothing more exciting for me than going to the movies.

My Aunt Mildred and Uncle Chestal took me to one of my earliest trips to the movie theater, where we watched *9 to 5*. After I saw Dolly on the screen, I wanted to hear everything this woman sang. I would later learn that my maternal grandmother's favorite female country singer was none other than Dolly Parton. And she too would help feed my new fascination for this newly discovered music.

Dad was upset with my newfound interest in country music and so more strictly enforced its banishment from our home. He did not like my aunt and uncle taking me (a three-year-old) to an adult movie. But I think what he disliked most was my new crush on a country music star. Needless to say, Aunt Mildred didn't take me to the movies anymore and the next film I saw was *Bambi!*

Grandma Stone, cousin Robin and Larry

With the taste of a different flavor of music in my mouth, I couldn't wait to visit both sets of grandmothers so they could play country music for me from their record collections. Grandma Ferguson played everything from Hank Williams, Kitty Wells, Ernest Tubb, and her personal favorites, Loretta Lynn and Elvis. It was on one of those visits another music style caught my ear, and little did I know that one day that music would become my life.

An avid Elvis Presley fan, Grandma Ferguson had every LP she could find of him and many of those records were Gospel. I loved all the upbeat Gospel numbers Elvis did, like *Swing Down Sweet Chariot Stop and Let Me Ride;* they made me feel something special. It wasn't until several years later I would learn what that special feeling was.

My parents divorced when I was six and I was now alone more than ever. Mom would have to throw herself into work to make ends meet, and to justify her time away from home, she showered me with toys, books and my favorite music. As she worked, I stayed with Grandma Stone, and she, of course, loved sharing her country music LPs with me. She also introduced me to *Hee-Haw* and *The Nashville Network*.

When I started singing some of the new Gospel songs I had learned from Grandma Ferguson's Elvis record, I saw a strange look on Grandma Stone's face. "No, we don't sing those songs," she said. "Those are songs they sing in your other Grandma's church. Those are Holy Roller songs. We just sing hymns in *our* church, so don't sing those or people will think you are a Holy Roller."

With my parents divorced, the rock-n-roll music rule no longer applied and we eventually started going to the Catholic Church. The

Grandma Ferguson and Larry

music in that church was different from the Gospel music I had heard on the Elvis record. It sure didn't make me feel anything special and it wasn't pleasing to sing or listen to as a child. But I couldn't trade it for the Gospel music I enjoyed because I didn't want to become a Holy Roller.

As I grew older, I became more and more discontent with the Catholic Church. I would fall asleep during Mass, pretend to be sick so I wouldn't have to go and even reset the alarm clock so Mom would oversleep. Now please understand, I love the Catholic people and as I have grown older, I have learned to appreciate their music. But as a young child, this music, as well as the ritualistic aspects of the services, didn't satisfy my longing for something different.

I was finally able to get out of Mass when a family friend, an elderly woman, asked my mother if she could hire me to stay with her at night. Ellen Loyd was like a grandmother to every child in our family, including our parents. My mother, and nearly all her sisters, had stayed at her home at night in case she fell. Ellen had broken her hip years ago and remained on a walker for the rest of her life. When I started staying with her, she was in her early 90's—although you couldn't tell it by her looks or actions. Although immobile, Ellen was strong in all other facets.

She was a member of the 18th Street Baptist Church, and since she was a shut-in, the church would visit her periodically. During one of those visits, someone invited me to go to Sunday School. Now, what young child wants to go to school? Let alone on Sunday? I finally agreed as my cousin, Cindy, had already been there and told me they gave her juice and cookies.

I attended the 18th Street Baptist Church for several years before one day feeling the wooing of the Holy Spirit. In a sense, it was the same feeling I felt when I listened to the Elvis Gospel record. Still a child, I went forward during the altar service and told the pastor I wanted to join the

Larry poses at age three

church. The pastor called a wonderful man named Earl Roth to come talk to me. Earl explained that joining the church was a great thought but to do so I had to be saved.

"Saved?" I said. "From what?"

"From Hell," Earl said.

Hell? What in the world have I done to deserve going to Hell? I was only a kid and didn't have time to do anything that bad! I had never killed anyone, stole anything. Why did this man think I was going to Hell? All sorts of thoughts ran through my mind. I thought Brother Earl was going to make me do something wild. Could he be one of those Holy Rollers my Grandma Stone told me about?

"Son, do you believe in Jesus Christ?" Earl asked.

"Yes!" I said.

Earl then took the Scriptures and shared the story of Nicodemus, who was a good man but still needed a Savior to be born-again. Earl went on to show me that everyone had sinned (even himself) and come short of the Glory of God. He explained that the wages of sin was death, and Christ came and died as my sacrifice. He went on to show me that through Christ's death and resurrection, we could be born-again spiritually. I gave my heart to Christ that night and things would change even more for me.

Each night when I entered Ellen's home, I found her watching preachers on a network called TBN. The network annoyed me with its screaming preachers and music Grandma Stone would have surely labeled as Holy Roller.

"Let's watch something else," I suggested.

"Oh no," Ellen said. "I have to watch this every night. This man is

Paul and his wife is Jan. I think she is so pretty and each night she wears a different bow in her hair."

"Oh please," I said, rolling my eyes. "This is horrible."

"Well this is *my* TV," Ellen said. "And we're watching *Praise The Lord!*"

Keep in mind I was just a young kid, not even a

Ellen Loyd and Larry

teenager. I was merely a saved Baptist boy warned against the crazy Holy Rollers out there. My music of choice was country and, of course, I loved singing Baptist hymns, as they weren't high church like the Catholic hymns.

Friends at church bought contemporary Christian and other styles of Gospel music for me, but it just didn't nourish me musically or spiritually. The elders in my church told me it was because I didn't want to give up the worldly country music and that secular music was sinful.

Terrified that Satan was influencing my soul because I listened to non-Gospel music, I prayed each night for the Lord to send Christian music to me that I would enjoy and wouldn't leave me torn.

One night while sitting by Ellen's chair, God answered my prayers as Paul and Jan, of TBN, hosted their *Praise The Lord* telecast. Annoyed as usual with Ellen for wanting to watch the Holy Rollers, I chuckled when they announced that one of their guests that evening was a woman with the last name of Rambo. I speculated as to how much ridicule this woman must receive with a last name like that.

The guest was Dottie Rambo and for some reason I took notice. I had never heard or seen this woman in my life, but that night I can still remember her singing *Oil and the Wine*, and playing her guitar singing, *Tears Will Never Stain the Streets of That City*. Ellen and I had never heard of these songs but found ourselves singing every word with the singer.

Our eyes hardly blinked as we listened to every word this tiny woman with the huge black hair sang. Without sensationalism, without gimmicks, this woman shared her faith and her music and we knew she was real. The Holy Spirit visited us and we were so naive in the Lord we didn't even know it.

From that moment on, I collected every recording I could find of Dottie Rambo. I remember the first Rambo's record I bought and took to church, telling everyone that Buck was Dottie's father and Reba was her sister. My church embraced my newfound music and explained that it wasn't Holy Roller music. It was pure Gospel music and that my Grandma

Stone, being Catholic and used to high church music, didn't understand there was nothing wrong with this music.

God used Dottie Rambo and her music to usher me into His presence and into His musical world of praise. He revealed to me that it was OK to enjoy singing His music and not just take part in a ritualistic hymn. His music could be for enjoyment as well as worship. He also showed me that in a Christian's life there was no such thing as secular and Gospel. A Christian is a Christian. If I listened to a clean country song, it was OK. God is the creator of all things and unless a song is contrary to Him or His teaching, we should not consider it a sinful song.

We must constantly look at life, music and even churches as though we're eating a wonderful fish dinner. We should enjoy all the good and nourishing portions, but we still have to look out for the bones. This is the attitude I have kept since my adolescence and God has blessed me for it.

When I think of my childhood, I see the many events as seeds sown, both intentionally and unintentionally, molding me into the person I am today. I'm amazed at how God works in our lives. Who would have ever thought that I would one day grow up to be a part of the life and ministry of the Gospel songbird sent that night to me while watching TBN?

Chapter 2
First Meetings

It is so very marvelous the way God puts people in our lives that truly make a difference for us.

—Barbara Mandrell

After learning that Dottie suffered from many spine surgeries, my wish to meet her only grew stronger. Many years and events had come and gone since first seeing her on television at Ellen's house. Now a grown man, married to my beautiful wife, Judy, I made it my goal to meet the woman who had so blessed my life.

Judy knew how much I wanted to meet Dottie, and we both feared her health could worsen before I would have the opportunity to tell her how much her music meant to my life. After learning Phil Cross had put together a special tribute concert in honor of Dottie and her music, we knew we had to go and meet this lady.

We arrived at the concert early and sat through many other singing showcases to insure a good seat in front. Determined to meet Dottie, I was like a detective searching for any sign of a tiny woman with big hair and big earrings. When I finally saw her, we quickly made our way toward her to talk with her.

"Ms. Dottie, do you mind if we take a photo with you?" I asked.

"I would love to take a photo with you," Dottie said. "But I have to warn you, I just painted my fingernails and

Judy and Larry on their wedding day in 1995

they're still wet, so if you mess 'em up I'll have to knock you down." I had no idea she had such a wonderful sense of humor.

Dottie felt Judy was too far back when she snapped the photo and suggested she try a closer shot. Dottie didn't realize I had a large telephoto lens on the camera, which was why Judy stood so far back. I never mentioned this to Dottie, as I was happy to get another chance to spend more time with my Gospel favorite. After the next photo, Dottie still felt Judy was too far back and suggested we take another.

"Now that's enough," Dottie's manager said (as I would have at this point). "The camera has a big lens and you have to get to the show."

"Do you take good photos with that camera?" Dottie asked me, ignoring her manager's advice. "I can tell it is expensive."

"Yes," I admitted. "I'm pretty good."

"Will you take a picture of me and my secretary?" she asked. "I can never get her to dress up, and now that she is, I want to be sure we get a picture!"

After snapping the requested photo, we enjoyed a powerful concert by the greatest names in Southern Gospel music—names such as Bill Gaither, Jake Hess, The Bishops, The Perry Sisters and many others. Dottie closed the show with *Come Spring* and the standing crowd wept, cheered and shouted.

From that moment on, I knew that one day I was going to work with this lady in some capacity.

Many have asked how I came to manage Dottie. Well the story is one most people would never have imagined. I was a concert promoter in Kentucky, and did some freelance booking for country and Gospel artists. My dream concert was to have an evening with Dottie Rambo.

After several failed tries, we set a date and I wanted this evening to be a success more than any concert I had ever promoted. This wasn't about making money; this was about blessing Dottie in a time when her public appearances were rare.

The concert was so successful the fire department nearly shut us down for having more people in the building than the fire codes allowed. It was a packed house, and people were sitting in the floor, in the aisles and lingering in the foyer and around the building. We turned away more than five hundred fans that night.

When Dottie graced the stage, the anointing of the Holy Spirit was stronger than I had ever witnessed. That's still what Dottie Rambo brings to the stage. When she enters the room, it becomes an event. Not many artists in Gospel music can make that claim.

From this evening on, Dottie and I developed a friendship. She became a spiritual mother, a friend and of course my hero in the faith. As our friendship became stronger, I began booking many of her concert dates. With me still living in Louisville and Dottie in Nashville, most of our contacts took place on the telephone or on the road.

One particular phone conversation will forever remain in my mind. Judy was pregnant with our first child, and her pregnancy was a bit late, but doctors assured us everything was fine. During an evening at home, our phone rang and on the other end was Dottie.

"Larry," Dottie said calmly. "Honey, I know this may sound odd and you may not understand, but the Lord impressed me to call you and tell you to get Judy to the hospital for something is wrong."

I have to admit I thought this was a bit unusual, but I trusted that this woman had heard from the Lord. Judy spoke with Dottie for a bit, explaining that she felt fine. We finally agreed to take her to the hospital and found out her blood pressure was rising to dangerous levels and the doctors immediately took action!

Dottie poses with Judy Ferguson

We were glad Dottie was obedient to what the Lord had told her and glad we listened to His warnings through His handmaiden. Later Judy gave birth to our son, Joseph Christian Bliss Ferguson (we call him Christian).

I booked Dottie to sing at our church (the 18th Street Baptist Church) a few months later, where she asked us to bring our little one onstage so she could pray for him. As she prayed, she said she could see him with a microphone in his hand while onstage in front of thousands of people.

"I'm not sure if he is to preach or sing," she said. "But I know God has His hand on this child and his life will touch many."

As she finished sharing this with the audience, Christian began reaching for the microphone. Judy, who was holding him, gently pulled his little hands away. Dottie asked her to allow him to take the microphone.

GranDot and Christian

"Maybe he will say his first words," she said.

"Ahh eww ahhh," came Christian's voice through the sound-system.

"See, he's already Spirit-filled and speaking in tongues," Dottie said with a smile. "Let him say something else. Can you say GranDot?"

"Dot!"   Christian screamed his first word in front of our church family.

Within a few weeks, Dottie faced a crisis in her ministry and needed to make some major decisions. After taking counsel from her friend and beloved assistant of over 20 years, Kate Collier, Dottie knew if she didn't take control over her life and ministry, she would soon die and her ministry would go with it.

As Dottie shared with me some of the problems and heartaches that I will not reveal in this book, (as these are for her to express and not me), my heart burned within me to somehow help her. Our family moved to Nashville, and I began managing both Dottie and her ministry soon afterwards.

In the recording studio

Chapter 3
Being GranDot

Some of my fondest memories are those surrounding my family and Dottie on the road between concert dates.

—Larry Ferguson

My wife, Judy, has been Dottie's personal assistant for the last three or four years. Judy is the glue that holds everything together. If Dottie needs earrings, Judy normally knows exactly which pair to get. If Dottie needs hosiery, Judy knows where to find it. It's as if these two women can read the other's mind.

One day Judy came in and said, "Dottie, I have to tell you something."

"Before you say it," Dottie said with a smile, "I already know what you are going to say: you're pregnant!"

With a sheepish grin, Judy shook her head while both laughed and cried with joy. For the next eight months, the two women made plans and wish lists for both Christian and the expected baby. While praying, Judy requested the Lord send a girl this time around. I, on the other hand, wanted a boy. We already knew what challenges were before us with a boy, and I thought the two guys could be buddies. I also knew I would be overprotective with a daughter.

Dottie's two-pound Yorkie, Shayde, was also in on the news. People are always asking me if Dottie is a DIVA. I can honestly say she is in *status*, but not in *attitude*. Shayde, on the other hand, *is* every bit a DIVA. Not only is she the star of the Rambo home, she is the smartest animal I have ever seen! When Dottie told Shayde Judy was pregnant, she ran over to Judy and sniffed her belly.

Throughout the pregnancy, Shayde would run to Judy's tummy and act as though she knew a baby was inside. We joked with her veterinarian about this and he told us a dog's hearing is much greater than ours and so Shayde could probably hear the baby.

Pierce Joshua came into this world after only eight months and God had blessed me with a second son. We take turns loving on him and spoil-

Judy, Larry, Christian and Pierce at Thanksgiving time.

ing him to pieces, and GranDot has enjoyed being active in every step of his life. She was there during the pregnancy and now keeps an eye on his early formative years.

Both Pierce and Christian love visiting GranDot. Between Shayde, Pierce and Christian, Dottie can't take a breath to relax. Dottie lines her bedroom with toys and allows the children to have a ball. Shayde is as big a child as Christian and Pierce, and all three have become lovable siblings. Christian and Pierce would rather play with Shayde than any human.

Dottie has adopted our Christian and Pierce as grandchildren and they have called her GranDot since they could speak. GranDot plays the doting grandmother well. Despite all she has to do in her life, and all she has had to deal with physically, she insists the children never visit a barber or hairstylist. No matter how hectic her life or career is, or how bad she may be feeling, when she sees either boy needing a trim or touchup, she immediately whips out her barber scissors.

Some of my fondest memories are those surrounding my family and Dottie on the road between concert dates.

I'll never forget the day we persuaded Dottie to visit an old-fashioned portrait studio in Gatlinburg, TN, to have photos made. Dottie and Christian dressed up in Harley Davidson gear and posed like bikers on a motorcycle. Afterwards, we dressed as hillbillies and had our family portrait made for our Christmas cards. Dottie was having the time of her life, relaxing and being herself. She really is a kid at heart.

As we played in costumes, word reached the Gatlinburg strip that Dottie Rambo was inside the portrait studio. Before we knew it, people filled the little studio taking photos and asking for autographs. The studio manager threatened to empty the building and close it until the end of our session, but Dottie stepped in. She promised the crowd of people that she would stay until each individual received an autograph or had a photo taken with her if they waited until we finished. Everyone agreed, but before the session ended, the crowd doubled in size. Therefore, Dottie posed for photos and signed autographs for the next hour and a half.

Christian, GranDot and Pierce spend a great deal of time together.

While still inside the studio, Christian and I jokingly invited Dottie to join us on the Gatlinburg Sky Lift. To our surprise, she agreed and off we went. Cameras snapped away as Dottie traveled up the mountain.

Special times like these are the side of Dottie most people never get to see. She is one of the most playful people you will ever meet when she gets free in her skin. Christian and Pierce usually bring out that freedom.

We often find Pierce with a brown face from Dottie feeding him fudgesicles. We are used to the sound of a strumming guitar as Dottie teaches them a new song or sings one of their favorites for them. Maybe even a *Do Re Mi Fa Sol La Ti Do,* as she teaches Christian how to stretch his vocal range.

Judy and the boys travel with us on many of the concert dates we drive to. It has become a ritual for Christian to duet with GranDot on *Stand by the River,* filling in for Dolly Parton, who originally recorded the number-one song with Dottie. It has been great for the product table as well because we sell more CDs of that title if Christian and GranDot sing it onstage. I guess the ole saying, *You can't go wrong with dogs or kids,* has some truth to it.

Chapter 4
Battle of the Bulge

Never wear a horizontal-striped shirt as it makes you appear wider than you are.

—Dottie Rambo

When I became Dottie's manager, I wasn't what you would call a thin man. I wasn't an excessively overweight one, either. Aided by the delicious fried chicken each Friday of Kate Collier (Dottie's friend and assistant of nearly 25 years before retiring) and the hotel room service while on the road, I started packing on the pounds.

When Judy and I married in 1995, I weighed 110 pounds. I probably gained that much *more* after my second year with Dottie! Anyone who knows me will tell you I am a hermit in some respects. So, while on the road, Dottie and I rarely get out. We usually stay in our respective rooms. This can get a little lonely and boring at times, and that extra call to room service eases the former unpleasantness and overcomes the latter.

You have seen offices where nearly every worker has a cup of coffee in their hand. This was never my case. My drink of choice was colas. I was never without one! When I decided to do something about my weight, I was drinking somewhere around thirty soft drinks a day. I think other than the taste of the drink I wanted the caffeine to give me that extra nudge through the day.

My weight didn't bother me, nor did it bother my wife. However, my knees started hurting and I was a little short of breath at times. I often found Dottie asking me, "Are you OK? You're walking funny."

Dottie has since told me she'd caught on to my weight gain early but didn't want to say anything. Looking back, I can now see that some of what she said or asked amounted to subtle hints—for example, "Do you drink diet or just regular soft drinks?"

When voting members inducted the late Vestal Goodman into the Kentucky Music Hall of Fame, they asked Dottie to present the induction. However, when Vestal passed away before the ceremony, the members asked Dottie to accept the award for Vestal and sing during her portion. A host of celebrities from all styles of music sat in the audience including

Tom T. Hall, Dwight Yoakam, Ricky Skaggs and members of the Backstreet Boys.

That night, someone took a photograph of Dottie, Kevin Richardson (Backstreet Boys) and me, and that photo changed my life. When I saw myself in the picture, I saw a person heading down the road to a heart

Dottie, Ricky Skaggs and Larry

attack! I looked like an enormous meatball! The Bible teaches us that we are to treat our body as the temple of the Lord. I had treated mine like the dumpster of a fast-food restaurant! I can make light of it now, but it was no joking matter then.

Dottie was there for me with encouragement like no one else. If I lost two pounds, she noticed and became my biggest cheerleader. She also gave me great tips— like never wear a horizontal-striped shirt as it makes you appear wider than you are. If you wear a vertical-striped shirt, it creates a slimming illusion. It really works! Therefore, only solid colors and vertical-stripes now fill my closet!

I began working out at the gym and took up the Atkins diet. After a month and a half, I had lost only ten pounds. Even with Dottie as my cheerleader, I started getting discouraged. I knew I couldn't continue the early morning and late-night workouts for the rest of my life. And I knew eating *only* meat wasn't going to wash, as I am

Vestal Goodman and Larry

not a huge meat-eater. I had to come up with a plan I could stick with for the rest of my life.

Dottie supplied more tips, like filling a gallon-sized milk container with water and drinking all the water throughout the day. This is a great way to flush your system of toxins and to fill your body up! With all that water, I guess the food has nowhere to go.

Dottie, Dwight Yoakam and Larry

When it comes to weight-control, Dottie is the most disciplined person I know. We constantly have to make her eat sweets and junk, as she lacks a sweet tooth and isn't a junk-food-junkie. If Dottie feels she is a pound or two too heavy, it will be gone before you know it.

Breads, potatoes and fried chicken are my sins of choice. If I had to give these up, I knew I would crash the diet. I knew to lose my weight, I was going to have to get a program that would last. So as I examined my lifestyle, I realized I wasn't a big eater. Soft drinks were my main con-

Dottie and Larry pose with Kevin Richardson, of the Backstreet Boys

sumption.

I never dreamed I could enjoy diet soft drinks, but I have learned to love them. So with Dottie's encouragement, some changed eating habits, and my new weapon of diet colas, I am a soldier winning the battle against the bulge. At the time of this writing, I have lost over eighty-five pounds.

It's hard to believe, but some people never noticed my weight loss. But throughout the whole ordeal, Dottie remained my biggest cheerleader and encourager. My wife was happy for me, but said I looked fine either way to her. It's good to know that if I decide to balloon again she doesn't mind!

To this day, Dottie has remained my biggest weight-loss fan and encourager. I have probably added a year or two to my life, and when God finishes healing Dottie's back, she may be able to carry me now!

The biography of Larry's battle of the bulge has a happy ending

Chapter 5
Kate Collier and the Stalker

After a few weeks, Dottie began noticing that many of her personal items started turning up missing each time Sister Susie paid a visit.

—Larry Ferguson

Moving to Nashville was an easy transition because we inherited an instant family with the move. Dottie became Christian's GranDot and Judy and I immediately connected with Kate Collier, who had taken care of Dottie and her home since the late sixties.

Filled with wisdom and the love of God, Kate Collier is a *beautiful* African-American with a smile so pure you could see and hear the Lord with every word she speaks. Her spirit brightens everyone she meets.

Kate made fried chicken that would melt in your mouth. Just thinking about it makes my mouth water while I'm writing this! In fact, Kate's fried chicken helped me gain many unneeded pounds that I later struggled to shed.

With everyone happy in our faithful bunch, we were able to work smoothly and peacefully. It's not too often you find this many people—with varying personalities and backgrounds—getting along as well as we did.

Kate and Dottie were close. I remember Kate sharing with me her experiences of first coming to work for Dottie. Occasionally Dottie had dinner parties where Kate took care of the kitchen and guests. Kate told me how Dottie would bring her out of the kitchen and introduce her to such luminaries as Jimmie Davis and J.D. Sumner. Kate said Dottie always introduced her as a friend and never a housekeeper.

The love between these women was obvious, and both extended that same love to my family. Kate's children and grandchildren became instant family to us as well. Her late daughter, Rochelle, would often visit and when she started in the door, she would yell, "Where's that crazy Larry?" Or, "Where's my boyfriend?" I couldn't wait to get a hug from Rochelle. Kate's granddaughter, Angel, was the same...an all-around good girl. Each took good care of Kate and they all loved their Aunt Dottie.

Kate was a wise counselor I depended on for many things. I would unload all my worries and problems on her, and she would listen and give sweet yet simple advice.

Through the good times and bad, we endured them all as a family and team. One of the worst things we went through together involved a deranged fan that I will refer to as *Sister Susie* (not her real name). Sister Susie had posed as a physical therapist and offered her services to Dottie as a ministry to bless her. Dottie—being as trustworthy as she is—took Sister Susie up on the offer, as she wanted to work on muscle tone and rebuild the strength she had lost because of her surgeries.

Sister Susie started out with one visit each week, and then moved them up to twice a week. Not long after that, we didn't know if she would ever leave! After a few weeks, Dottie began noticing that many of her personal items started turning up missing each time Sister Susie paid a visit.

On one particular evening, Sister Susie—for reasons I can't remember—took our company van out for a drive. When I came to the office the next morning, I noticed the van had been in an accident. Kate had beaten me to the office that day and had noticed the wreckage as well.

When confronted, Sister Susie tried to blame *me* for the wrecked van! We had only one set of keys to the van and Dottie knew Sister Susie was the last to drive it—not to mention, Kate had made it into the office that morning before I arrived and knew I couldn't have done it. God had protected me, but we knew we were dealing with some troublesome spirits.

We later learned that Dottie's personal effects (shoes and such) were not the only items missing; her driver's license, social security card and other identification cards were disappearing somehow. Dottie immediately changed the locks and alarm codes to her home and offices. However, Sister Susie never gave up, forcing Dottie to change her telephone numbers.

As we started out on the road doing small tours, Sister Susie would appear at the concerts and services. Dottie told us to keep Sister Susie as far away from her as possible. This had turned into full-blown stalking, and now I became even more of the enemy in Sister Susie's mind as I shielded Dottie from her.

One particular tour stretch put us in Gatlinburg for several days. After checking Dottie into her room and making sure everything was secure, Judy, Christian and I decided to spend the rest of the afternoon enjoying the rides and amusements in the area. While on the road, we heard someone honk-

GranDot with Christian Ferguson

ing a car horn repeatedly. As I looked around, I noticed Sister Susie driving in the next lane and motioning for me to pull over.

"Yes?" I asked after pulling to the side of the road.

"I thought maybe we could go get a bite to eat," she said.

"Well," I said with hesitation, "we are on our way to Dollywood."

"Oh," she said with a disappointed sigh. "Well I can't afford to pay for Dollywood. I'll have to pass." She started to leave, then turned back to me. "Hey, I have some items I need to return to you. Do you mind if I give you a call in your room later and bring them by?"

"That would be great," I said, hoping she would return the missing items.

Dottie at an impromptu autograph signing

"OK," she said with a fake smile. "What room are you in?"

"212," I said awkwardly.

We left and enjoyed a day of fun with the many rides and activities Pigeon Forge and Gatlinburg have to offer. However, on the way home, I couldn't help but ponder our conversation with Sister Susie.

"How did she know which hotel we stayed at?" I said to Judy. "She asked for the room number but not the name of the hotel."

We realized that this woman had followed us. After all, how did she just happen to be in the lane next to us? Before we got back to the hotel, we surmised that Sister Susie had called the hotel operator and asked for Larry Ferguson's room—not 212 but the *other* room. True to our suspicions, Sister Susie had done everything we feared she would do.

Dottie was uncomfortable with her clever methods of tracking us down, yet this time Dottie decided to talk with her.

Judy, Pierce and Christian spend Christmas with GranDot at her home.

Not only did Dottie talk with Sister Susie, she had the presence of mind to record the conversation. What most people don't realize is how smart and easily adaptable Dottie can be when it comes to discerning spirits.

When I got to her room, Dottie had just hung up with Sister Susie. I explained how naive I was to allow this woman to trick me into giving Dottie's whereabouts.

"Honey, don't worry," Dottie said. "She wanted to talk with me and she sure got her wish!"

Dottie played the recording for me, revealing Dottie's insistence that Sister Susie return her personal items and keep her distance. To my surprise, Sister Susie agreed to leave Dottie alone and respect her privacy.

However, this same woman showed up again at the concert that evening. However, another fan—claiming to have worked with Sister Susie in the past—warned us that we had no idea of the potential danger we could be in. By the end of the night, security guards escorted Sister Susie out of the building for unknown reasons.

I realized then that some fans show up as wolves in sheep's clothing. I also realized the dangers a celebrity goes through daily. Even an anointed Gospel singer is not free from becoming a stalker's prey.

Chapter 5
Humorous Short Stories

Jump in for the joyride ... a journey of laughter and reflections...and best of all, everybody gets a window seat and Larry pays for the gas!!! *Bless his heart.*

—Aaron Wilburn

Because celebrities live and work under public scrutiny, they are always subject to humiliation and embarrassment.

Singers and musicians are a lot like trapeze artists: they live life on the high-wire. If they should fall, everyone is witness. Some audience members will cheer and some will focus solely on how the artist recovers from mistakes.

Dottie's sense of humor and quick wit has saved her from many embarrassing moments though the years.

Holy Woman

As any diehard fan knows, Dottie Rambo removes her shoes sometime during the concert and, after performing a few recent hits, takes requests while performing classics with just a guitar. One night while Dottie was going into the guitar portion of the program, a woman in the audience yelled, "Dottie, you have a hole in your panty hose!"

Quick at the draw, Dottie looked down at her hose and said, "Ah, I sure do. Well, I'm a *Holy* woman!"

Runaway Beads

On another occasion, Dottie explained to the audience that she needed to get comfortable and removed her earrings and wristwatch. "Don't worry," she said, jokingly. "That is far as I am going!" At that moment, every bead on her gown fell apart! "Catch them!" Dottie shouted. "I'm going to get my money back for this sucker!"

Dottie has fun with Christian and Pierce. It seems Pierce has temporarily taken over the song.

The Concerned Fan

Sometimes the humor is behind-the-scenes. Dottie performed *Too Much to Gain to Lose* with the Martins while filming a Gaither video at the Saenger Theatre in New Orleans, Louisiana. She wore a beautiful envelope collared, baby blue suit and was the picture of class...so we thought.

After the video's release, we received a letter from an Indiana woman expressing her joy at seeing Dottie on the Gaither program. However, she also mentioned her concern of Dottie's appearance.

> *I knew something was wrong when I saw you on the Gaither video, the woman wrote. When I saw you come out in that cheap suit instead of the beautiful beaded gowns you have always worn, I knew someone had robbed you blind and you were struggling. Here's two hundred dollars; please go buy yourself something beautiful!*

Dottie and I laughed afterwards because no artist wears beaded gowns at a Gaither video shoot. Concerned about the letter, Dottie asked

Larry, Dottie and Claude Hopper, founder of the Hoppers, share a lighthearted moment on the Gospel stage.

what we should do.

"Next time wear blue jeans," I joked. "Maybe the woman will send more money!"

The Name Game

One night Dottie was doing a show with then up-and-coming Southern Gospel artists, the Crabb Family. The promoter had worked hard getting the word out and the response was great. Some of his advertising efforts were obvious when we pulled into the city the day of the concert. Within a mile of the city limits, we saw a huge billboard that read, *TONIGHT DOTTIE RAMBO WITH THE CRABBS!*

Dottie gave me a solemn look and said, "I think I would change my name if I were the Crabb Family." She paused a moment and smiled. "And I might have to change *my* name after word gets out about this sign!"

P.D.

Songwriting seminars are always an experience. One particular night a novice songwriter brought up the subject of P.D., which stands for *public domain*. "In all the hymnals I see songs listed as P.D.," the man said. "What does that mean?"

"That's easy," Dottie said, flashing a playful grin. "P.D. stands for *Pay Dottie!*"

Chapter 6
Tulsa, Branson and Jim Bakker

I have known Larry "In The Line Of Duty" or should I
say on the job for a few years now. I have found him
to be the utmost professional. .

—Stella Parton

In recent years, I've had a sidekick for our travels. Our webmaster,
Chris Barnes, has begun traveling with Dottie and me, taking care of the
merchandise and anything else we can throw his way. Chris is my best
friend and a jack-of-all-trades. A young college student, he is eager and

willing to learn or try
anything. I think an
experience Chris will
never forget is one of
his first flights with
us.

This particular
trip would have us
flying to Tulsa,
Oklahoma, for a con-
cert at the ORU
Mabee Center, and
then a short drive to
Branson, Missouri,

Larry and Chris Barnes cut-up after a concert date.

for a concert and an appearance on the Jim Bakker show. Chris hadn't
flown with us much at this point, and was still learning everything.
Dottie's mothering instinct had made Chris feel welcome and a part of the
team. Dottie talked with Chris, swapping stories and giving insight to
keep him at ease, insuring he felt part of our traveling caravan.

About halfway into our flight, a stirring took place a few seats ahead
of us. After a few moments, we heard enough second-hand conversation
to know a man in front of us was ill. Soon after learning the news, the pilot
asked for any doctors or nurses on board to report to where the man was
sitting. Within minutes, a few people stretched him out on the floor and
gave him CPR.

Within a matter of minutes, the man (who had been just a few feet away from us) had now left this world and passed on to the next. This incident disturbed us and for the rest of the flight left us with much to think about. But for the grace of God, this could have been one of us. This man was traveling alone—no one knowing of whom to contact for him, no familiar face to be with him in his last minutes. Having no other choice but to witness this man as he left his earthly shell was a turning point in our lives that changed our hearts and minds forever.

"Kids, listen to what I say," Dottie said in soft tone. "Every night check off your laundry-list and make things right with God. Ask Him to forgive even your secret sins you're unaware of because you never know when it's your time to go."

After a great night in Tulsa, Oklahoma, we headed to Branson, Missouri. People from all over the country travel to Branson for nightly shows headlined by national acts. Gospel, Country, Easy Listening and Show tunes are all a part of the lineup. Promoters booked Dottie to sing at the Mel Tillis Theater for the Annual Jubilee Conference. While in town, she was to film an episode of her dear friend Jim Bakker's television program.

Arriving at the hotel late and hungry, we didn't have much choice as to where we would eat. Our driver had left with our car and Chris, and I had to settle for a meal at the local Denny's! I know you think life on the road is glamorous, and that we just pick, sing, and chow down on lobster. Not so. To be honest, Chris and I should own stock in Denny's, Steak'n'Shake and Waffle House as they are usually the only eateries open after a day of preparing and completing a concert.

Waiting for our food in a Denny's booth, I noticed a young woman coming in the door making direct eye contact with me. I thought she had recognized me from one of Dottie's concerts and was coming over to say hello, or inquire about the upcoming Branson appearances. The young woman came to our booth and nearly sat in my lap. I quickly realized she wasn't a Dottie Rambo fan, but just a girl who was under the influence of spirits. I'm speaking of the kind that comes in a bottle, not the Holy one. As we would say in Nashville, she was *slop-drunk*.

"Hi!" she said and began drinking my Diet Coke.

"Well how do you do? Just help yourself," I said with a slap of sarcasm.

"Do you know who my mom is?" she asked.

"No," I said as if speaking to a five-year-old, "but my grandpa is Pat Boone if that makes a difference."

"I don't know him," she said.

"But do you know who my mom is?" she said.

"No, I don't."

This young woman revealed that her mother was a well-known Christian in the entertainment world. I then felt embarrassment for both her mother and this young woman who obviously wrestled with many demons in her life.

Dottie and Larry visit with Jim Bakker in Branson

"Does your mom know you are drinking like this?" I asked.

She gave me a defensive look and said, "I'm drunk; so what?"

This young woman ignored our attempts to sober her up, and because of her continued actions, the manager finally asked her to leave. I felt so bad that she had to battle her issues alone, possibly harassing some innocent bystander who may not have been as kind as Chris and I.

The next morning, Jim Bakker sent a car to take us to his studios. Dottie was eager to see Jim and his wife, Lori, as she had only seen him once in the last 17 years. Dottie has worked with Jim since the televangelist's ministry was in its infancy. She is also an avid viewer of his program, normally staying up until three AM to watch the late run of his show.

An enthusiastic Jim and Lori Bakker greeted us. Jim had asked Dottie, Chris and me if we would like to take a new personality test his ministry had worked with. We agreed and learned quite a bit about our personalities.

Jim looked over the results in shock. Without going into much detail, the results showed the three of us were so different that our personalities needed each other. Dottie's results revealed she needed alone time and enjoyed being in crowds only to give of herself. It revealed that although she wanted total control of her personal life, she preferred someone making major business decisions on her behalf. Mine revealed that I loved to be in crowds on my terms and likewise needed alone-time and preferred to lead in my personal and business life without trying to control another person. Chris's personality revealed that he liked following someone else's leadership and loved to be in large crowds and was rarely left alone.

For the rest of the trip we teased one another about Dottie being normal, me being bossy, and Chris being a slave! We learned a lot on this trip—about or mortality, about our purposes and friendships—and about dining in a late-night eatery, which is: prepare for anything!

Chapter 7
Lily Tomlin

Larry Ferguson fell into our lives like a penny from Heaven.

—Lily Tomlin

Dottie and I have met several people along our journey that have become special friends. One particular family stands out in my mind more so than most. Our meeting of these wonderful folks came from a most unlikely circumstance.

As we returned home from a press conference with Kentucky Governor Ernie Fletcher, Dottie began to feel a bit under the weather. By the time we made it back to Nashville, she was ill enough for me to rush her to the emergency room. While Dottie waited in a chair by the waiting room door, I searched for a wheelchair because the hospital can be a long walk for anyone, sick or well.

As I quickly searched for a wheelchair, one of the hospital attendants stopped me and said, "You look lost, how may I help you?"

"Well, I need a wheelchair," I said. "Do you know where I might find one?"

"You look like you're getting around fine to me," he said. "Who is it for?"

"Her," I said, p o i n t i n g   t o   a   disheveled figure sitting in the waiting room. I didn't mention h e r   n a m e because Dottie was in her housecoat and nightgown, wearing no makeup and her hair up in a turban.

"Oh my," the man said. "That's Dottie Rambo!"

"She wants to remain anonymous," I said, following the attendant as he headed toward her.

"Ms. Rambo, my name is Michael Langston," he said. "I am going to sneak you on back and there won't be a soul that needs to know who you are." A broad smile stretched across his face. "I have listened to your music all my life. Why, I know the lyrics to all your songs and can quote, word-for-word, every story you've told on TBN."

I first thought Michael was just being polite, but within minutes, I realized he was a true-blue Dottie Rambo fan. He gave details from her stories and recited song lyrics to some of her biggest hits. He was more than a fan that day, however; he was an angel in human form.

He told about growing up in Paducah, KY, where his whole family loved Dottie Rambo. He also told us about his lifelong friend, Lillie Mae Tomlin.

"Lillie Mae and I watch you on TBN and she loves your music," he said. "Her children, Richard and Lily Tomlin, love you, too."

"Lily Tomlin?" I asked, "the actress?"

"Yes," Michael said. "That's her."

He explained that Lillie Mae was 91 years old and bedridden after a backbreaking fall in her home. When he spoke of the woman, his eyes twinkled, revealing love and admiration. We later discovered she was a second mother to him in many ways.

"I know we just met," he said. "But if you'll allow me to exchange phone numbers with Larry, I would gladly introduce you to Lillie Mae." Tears welled in Michael's eyes. "I know that it would lift her spirits if you could drop by and pray with her."

"I would love to do that," Dottie said without hesitation.

Ms. Dottie was back on her feet after a week or so and answered the phone when Michael called inviting us to Lillie Mae's home. He mentioned that both her children, Richard and Lily, would be there and wanted to meet us as well. Little did we know this visit would bring one of the sweetest families into our lives.

Lillie Mae may have been bedridden, but her mind was as sharp as a tack. "Mercy, you can't be Dottie Rambo," she said when introduced to Dottie. "Dottie Rambo should be flat of her back or in a chair, not up walking around!" This was all the proof I needed that this woman had watched TBN all those years, keeping informed about Dottie's terrible back surgeries.

After visiting with Lillie Mae, Michael,

Larry, Dottie, Lily Tomlin and Judy

Richard and Michael's mother, Joyce Sedeberry, who was also Lillie Mae's nurse, a soft touch on my shoulder made me turn, finding Lily's beautiful smile.

"Hi, Larry, it is so good to meet you," she said, turning her attention to Dottie. "Oh, Dottie, what an honor, thank you so much for coming to see Mom."

Now you have to realize as a child, my favorite movie was *The Incredible Shrinking Woman*, and the first movie I saw in a theater was *9 to 5*, so meeting Lily Tomlin was a big deal to me.

I'm usually good about containing myself, but that night I wanted to jump out of my skin and shake myself to make sure I wasn't dreaming. I couldn't get over how beautiful she was in person. Her skin is flawless, without having aged a minute since her days of *Laugh In*.

Dottie and I talked and mingled with everyone, but it didn't take long for Lillie Mae to steal our hearts. "You know I used to sing in a Gospel quartet, don't you," she said.

"I didn't know that," Dottie replied. "What part did you sing?"

Lillie Mae smiled. "Bass," she said as the room filled with laughter.

"I see where Lily gets her humor," Dottie said, still laughing.

"Well, maybe so," said Lillie Mae. "But she's the one getting paid for it!"

Line after line, this precious woman entertained us with short stories and funny jokes. Michael finally broke in, asking Lillie Mae if she would like Dottie to pray with her. Lillie Mae assured that she would and we gathered around her bedside as Dottie prayed a simple sweet prayer.

We had a light meal afterwards with Richard, Lily and Michael at Richard's house. Richard is a talented man in his own right; he can sing, dance, act, and is an incredible painter, cook and interior designer. To be honest, there isn't much he can't do.

It was great to sit back and listen to Lily

Lily Tomlin, Dottie, Michael Langston and Richard Tomlin

and Dottie as they talked. For two people coming from such extreme opposites of the entertainment world, they sure found a great deal of common ground. At one point, Michael leaned over to me and said, "Well the Queen of Gospel and the Queen of Comedy are sure hitting it off well."

Lily listened intently as Dottie told stories about her ministry and life on the road. We shared many of the stories found in this book, and listened as Lily talked about her career and the characters she had turned into pop culture icons.

Several weeks later, Dottie hosted the *Ernest Tubb Midnight Jamboree*, which is a live radio show following the Grand Ole Opry each Saturday night. About a week before the Jamboree, Michael called to tell me he and Richard had dinner with Lily the previous night.

"Richard and I wore our Dottie Rambo buttons," he said. "Lily asked for one and she wore it all night."

Before hanging up, Michael said, "Oh, I wanted to tell you that Lily is joining us at the Midnight Jamboree to see Dottie."

My jaw dropped. "Are you serious?"

"Yeah, when she found out we were going, she asked to come, too," he said. "She's making a movie with Bob Altman called *A Prairie Home*

Dottie sings at the Ernest Tubb Midnight Jamboree

Companion and the script calls for her singing country and Gospel music, so she may use the opportunity to study Dottie."

When I picked up Lily, Michael and Richard, I noticed all three of them were still wearing their Dottie Rambo buttons. This, of course, brought a smile to Dottie's face, which always puts a smile on mine.

At that time, our youngest child, Pierce, would never allow anyone other than me, Judy, GranDot or close family members hold him. But that night, when Lily walked over to say hello to him and Judy, he took right to her. We captured the moment in a photograph, and after getting into Lily's arms, Pierce didn't want to go back to Mama.

As Dottie performed during the program, she asked me, Lily, Michael and Richard to join her onstage to help with a couple songs. Of course, Dottie persuaded Lily into playing a few characters for the audience, such as Ernestine, the telephone operator, and everyone's favorite smarty-pants 5-year-old: Edith Ann.

Singing backup to *I Go To The Rock* and *Stand By The River*, Lily was dancing and clapping along, all the while turning to me saying, "I just love this music and this band!" Meeting the President of the United States could not have topped that moment for me.

Lily not only studied Dottie that night, she also took in every aspect

Lily Tomlin and Pierce Ferguson become instant buddies

of the music. To be honest, Lily took in everything in the room. Gifted with an ingenious perception of human characteristics, Lily does not simply invent a character; she breathes life into people we cherish—or laugh at—forever.

A couple of weeks later, Lily called, requesting several of Dottie's videos. She explained that while filming *Prairie Home Companion*, she wanted to study how the Gospel singing families interacted while performing.

Michael later helped Dottie find a new home, as well as Judy and me. He is one of those people who know everyone, and if he doesn't know them, he knows someone who does. If you run into a snag, Michael is the first person you call.

While moving into our new homes, Dottie slipped on some of the moving materials and broke one of her legs—a femur to boot. We immediately rushed her to the hospital, where she endured surgery and extensive rehabilitation.

Richard and Michael were guardian angels for us during this time. Both men jumped to our aide with decorating, moving, unpacking and just about everything in between. Friends like these men are rare.

Lily called us on several occasions, checking on Dottie's recovery. Dottie received a package one morning and asked me to open it. Inside, we found an Edith Ann doll with a note from Lily saying, "Since I couldn't be with you, I sent Edith Ann to watch over your recovery!" I bought Dottie an oversized rocking chair just like the one Edith had on *Laugh In*. It still puzzles me how a movie star in the middle of filming a major motion picture could take the time to check on Dottie. To me, that is the true heart of a Good Samaritan.

While Dottie's recovery continued, Lillie Mae's health worsened. This precious woman had made mention she wanted Dottie to sing at her funeral, so when Michael called telling us that God could take her home at any moment, he mentioned that everyone would understand if Dottie couldn't sing since she was still recovering. Dottie made me assure everyone she would be there, singing for Lillie Mae's service, even if she had to do so from a wheelchair.

Not long after that, Lillie Mae passed away and Dottie made it to the funeral, singing *Sheltered In the Arms Of God* and *Mama's Teaching Angels How To Sing*. It was the most beautiful service I have ever attended.

Richard sang *I'll Be Seeing You* and brought tears to everyone's eyes, as did Lily's comments about her mother. One special moment came when Lily mentioned that her mother delighted in always letting Lily know she

Lily and Larry

was the original Lillie Tomlin. I won't go into more detail about the service as it is a private matter for the family, but I will say that there were many people who loved Lillie Mae.

The love that poured out to us from all the people at the funeral was beyond description. One of the sweetest moments was when family member, Jane Wagner, said to me, "You're family now!" I thought that was so kind, coming from her at such a disheartening time.

I do feel like the Tomlins are indeed family. I couldn't ask for any better friends than these folks. Michael and Richard are like brothers to me, and I hope they feel the same. In fact, Richard gave me one of his original paintings for my birthday, and I treasure its beauty and significance.

Another of my most treasured possessions is a birthday gift from Lily. She had the entire cast of *Prairie Home Companion* autograph the movie poster and sent the sweetest handwritten note for my birthday. That's the type of person Lily Tomlin is. Despite years of playing an assortment of characters, she is a real person and one that hasn't forgotten what it means to be real.

When I was 10 years old, I begged my mother to take me to the McCauley Theater (now the Brown Theater) in Louisville, KY to see Lily perform her *Search For Signs Of Intelligent Life* show. At the end of the performance, I was the first person in the balcony to stand in ovation and Lily started blowing kisses to me, saying, "To that little boy in the balcony, thank you. Thank you."

When I think about that night so many years ago, I always smile at the thought that she is now a special person to us. Thank you Lily Tomlin for being so loving to me and to my family. If we had more people like you, the world would be a much better place, and as Edith Ann would say, "And that's the truth!"

My oldest son, Christian, had a teacher send a note home from school after the entire class watched the Magic School Bus, a cartoon in which Lily is the voice of Mrs. Frizzle. The teacher wrote how Christian's imagination sometimes worried her because he insisted he knew Mrs. Frizzle. She went on to tell us in the note that we should let him know that Mrs. Frizzle isn't real.

Ah, if the woman only knew how real she is!

Chapter 8
Fans and Fanatics

What an awesome thing it is to see someone dedicate their life, mostly behind the scene, to keep this great ministry going.

—Gerald Crabb

Meeting people all over the world has been an adventure! It's interesting how people can be so much alike, yet so different at the same time. I didn't realize how true this was before dealing with Dottie's fan-base. Not only does she have some of the most loyal fans in Gospel music, she has the most diverse group of fans I have ever seen. People from all walks of life love and respect this woman.

In our travels around the country, I have met folks who have followed Dottie's ministry from before her marriage or first record deal. I met one couple who attended the first revival Dottie held in Indiana when she left home at 12 years of age. It's encouraging that people like that have remained loyal after all that time.

Some are typical Southern Gospel fans who enjoy everyone from the McKameys, Dove Brothers and Crabb Family to all the older groups like the Blackwoods and Statesmen. Others have loved her since the 80's, when she was blazing musical roads that led to the beginnings of the Inspirational and Contemporary Christian movement. Many are country music fans who grew up in the church but now never attend.

Little girls have always loved Dottie, writing letters to her expressing how they wanted to be like her when they grew up. The African-American community has treated Dottie as if she were royalty. Nearly every visit to the airport we find ourselves surrounded by these beautiful people more so than any other category of fans.

After the release of Dottie's *Stand by the River* CD—her first solo project in well over a decade—we noticed a big shift in Dottie's fan-base. More and more young people began attending her concerts and signings. One of Dottie's largest CD signings took place with nearly every person in the line being college age or younger males.

Dottie is one of the most accommodating celebrities I know when it comes to her fans. Even with all her past back problems, she still signs autographs after every show. Sometimes she has stayed at a booth or autograph table for up to five hours signing and greeting fans. With every person that passes before her, she tries to leave them with a memory of love and kindness. I have seen many younger or more able-bodied artists isolate themselves from their fan-base.

This isn't to say that being the object of a fan's affection is always delightful. Neighbors from Dottie's last address watched as two people wearing Dottie Rambo T-shirts stole Dottie's garbage cans! When I asked why the neighbors didn't stop them or call the police, the sweet woman said, "Well, since they were wearing Dottie's T-shirts, we thought they were part of her staff!"

After I told Dottie what had happened, she laughed it off by saying, "Well they sure aren't going to get a good souvenir from that! It's a shame they got my new cans though!"

Once on a whim, Dottie decided she wanted to go to the Opry Mills Mall in Nashville, as she had never shopped there. She and I went alone

Dottie's daughter, Reba Rambo-McGuire, tenderly holds Pierce

Could it be that Larry secretly wants to be the next Chet Atkins?

and it was so much fun seeing Dottie in a shopping mood. As we passed one of those store chains where every item is only a dollar, Dottie decided she would like to see if the store had toys she could buy for her puppy, Shayde.

While waiting in the checkout line, the woman in front of us turned to Dottie and said, "Ma'am, may I ask you a question?"

"Sure," Dottie said with a smile.

"Do you think it would be tacky if I put these pink flowers on my husband's grave?" The woman nodded to the artificial flowers in her arms. "Do you think he would find them too sissified?"

"Ahh, honey," Dottie said. "I don't think he will mind at all what you do with those flowers."

The woman suddenly dropped both arms of flowers, screamed out a profanity and said, "Oh my (BLEEP BLEEP BLEEP), you're that Dottie Rambo!"

Later, while still in the mall, I needed to visit the men's room. I never leave Dottie alone in public as fans sometimes swamp her. Many of these folks merely want to love on Dottie, but most never realize how tiny she is and how painful a pat on the back can be from a six-foot man. However, this time I had to find a quiet place for Dottie to wait until I returned from the restroom. When I came out, I found her behind an autograph line in the Opry Mills food court, signing everything from napkins to paper plates! Dottie gave each fan a memory they will cherish.

Some fans mean well but can take things a bit too far. Once when Dottie was in the hospital, a strange lady came to my home and refused to leave until I took her to visit Dottie at the hospital. There was no way I was going to take a stranger to see Dottie, especially one that demanding. Finally, after many refusals, the lady left. While on my way to visit Dottie at the hospital, I stopped at a local grocery store and noticed the woman was following me on the opposite ends of every aisle. I realized she was more than just a persistent fan and made sure she lost me in the parking lot.

Many situations like this arise, but Dottie handles it all in stride. If every artist took the time Dottie takes with her fans, I'm sure most fans would leave satisfied and fulfilled. I know from my own experience, after you have waited years to meet a celebrity you admire, you hope it will be a positive memory. It's not idol worship ... *merely admiration.*

A lady in the ministry once told me she didn't socialize with her fans because the recognition was God's and not hers. I totally agreed with her that God uses humans to carry His message, and sometimes they take credit for what *He* does. But I also pointed out that certain books of the Bible are named after godly men and women for a reason. God will not share His Glory, but He wants His children to love and appreciate the work He created, not only in a beautiful landscape but also in humanity.

Chapter 9
Well Hello Dolly

Larry is a wonderful man that I'm proud to call a friend.

—Dolly Parton

There are only a handful of celebrities with enough star-power to bolster a first-name-only relationship with fame. Dolly Parton is at the top of this list, with icon status in the music industry and beyond. If I were to say, "I just love Dolly," or "Dolly's new song is great," you would know (without needing a last name) I was referring to the undisputed Queen of Country Music.

Dolly has a presence of comfort and ease that makes even total strangers feel as though they have been friends with her for years. In many ways, she and Dottie are a lot alike. Both are award-winning songwriters. Both are industry trailblazers. And both are incredible performers with limitless talent and quick wit.

Dottie and Dolly have known each other since both moved to Nashville in the 1960s. Early days would have the future legends passing in restaurants and eventually setting up offices in neighboring buildings. Dottie occasionally appeared on the *Porter Wagoner Show* (which, quite frankly, should have been named the *Dolly Parton Show*) so a friendship between the two women developed early on.

As their careers moved forward and success embraced both women, meetings between the two became fewer and fewer. Toward the end of the 1980s, with Dottie's health problems and spine deterioration, the women lost all contact. This is common in the music industry as artists are busy with careers that take them all over the world.

From the time I began traveling with Dottie as her manager, I have listened as countless fans and musicians inquired about the possibility of Dottie and Dolly recording a song together. To this day, we get more questions about Dolly than any other artist Dottie has worked with.

Many years passed since the two had seen each other when the promoters of a huge Gospel Music convention in Pigeon Forge invited Dottie to perform for a special television program. While there, the organization honored Dottie with a banquet where many famous preachers, like Jerry

Judy, Dolly, Larry and Christian

Falwell, sat in the audience. Another honoree at the luncheon was Dolly Parton's aunt, evangelist Dorothy Jo Owens, whom Immanuel Baptist College awarded an honorary Doctorate in Sacred Music.

Dolly sent a prerecorded video for this ceremony, congratulating her aunt on this special occasion; and as she made her closing remarks in the video, Dolly took the time to send a special message to Dottie as well.

"How sweet," Dottie said, turning to me with a smile. "I would love to see her again."

My promotions company was a corporate sponsor for one of Dolly's charities, *The Dolly Parton Imagination Library.* Each year, Dolly invites sponsors to a special performance at Dollywood and welcomes everyone to a private reception for a quick photo op. So I asked Dottie to accompany my wife, Judy, and me for this special night.

I had met Dolly before this event but there is always something exciting about being around her. If you don't have a smile on your face when Dolly enters the room, I promise you will be wearing one before she leaves. Dolly has a God-given talent for making anyone around her happy. Whether from a quick joke or an uplifting song, her smile softens even the hardest of hearts and disarms anyone in contact with her.

It was the Christmas season and Dolly made her entrance dressed in a Santa Claus outfit. I daresay Santa should count it a blessing that Mrs. Claus isn't half the looker as Dolly or the elves would never get those toys made!

Dolly's face lit up when she saw Dottie on the other side of the stage. With hands glued to the sides of her face, she ran to embrace her long lost friend.

"Girl, what are you doing here?" Dolly asked with a girlish squeal. "Honey your skin is just beautiful, what do you use?"

"Alexandra de Markoff."

"You're still using that?" Dolly said with her schoolgirl charm. "I guess I should have kept using it!"

Dolly's skin is flawless with the complexion of a porcelain doll, so this

Dottie, Ms. Santa (Dolly) and Larry

was a high compliment. By the end of the night, the two women had caught up on the lost years and I had the opportunity to steal a hug from the Queen of Country Music.

Dottie decided to record her first album since recovering from several back surgeries and asked Dolly if she would join her in a duet for the project. Dolly agreed and we mailed her a selection of songs from which she could choose to record. While creating the review CD, one song accidentally made its way to the submission—and wouldn't you know it, Dolly handpicked that song, *Stand by the River*, for the duet.

"Larry, I don't remember that one," Dottie said to me with a laugh. "Are you sure I wrote it?"

"Yes, I'm sure," I said. "You don't remember it?"

"Well when you write as many songs as I have,"

Dottie and Dolly sing together

Dottie said, still laughing, "you see if *you* can remember them all!"

Several weeks before the women would record their vocals, Dottie suffered the beginnings of a terrible cold. Even as her condition worsened, Dottie assured me she was fine and did not need to go to the doctor.

One morning, while I was working out of Dottie's home office, Kate (Dottie's assistant) told me that Ms. Dottie was resting so well she did not try to awaken her.

Since her surgeries, Dottie has not been able to sleep for more than a couple of hours at a time, so we were not about to interrupt this rare span of rest. Kate continued with her daily routine, as did I until around 3:30 in the afternoon. "Surely she isn't still sleeping," I said to Kate. "She's never rested this long before."

A few minutes later, Kate rushed into my office and told me she couldn't wake Dottie. After several failed tries, I quickly called 911 and an ambulance soon came. Dottie was in a coma and before paramedics could get her to the ambulance, her heart had stopped and they quickly worked to revive her. I couldn't believe this was happening.

The doctor said her situation was serious and he could make no promises. However, I knew deep in my heart that she was going to pull through because I have never met a stronger person than Dottie Rambo. The next morning she was awake and ministering to all the nurses and aides surrounding her.

I'm not going to go into great detail about the coma, as I'm sure Dottie will do so in her memoirs. However, I needed to mention it to show how determined she was to record her duet with Dolly. In fact, we received a special early release from the hospital so she could be at the recording studio.

This woman truly lives the lyrics of one of her songs: *Defeat is one word I don't use.* She could have easily waved a flag of surrender, yet moved forward, putting all her trust in God. And ready or not, she was leaving the hospital because she had a project to record.

Dottie was not about to let Dolly see her hooked up to an oxygen tank, so shortly before the Queen of Country Music arrived, Dottie made me hide the tank and respirator behind a large sofa in the studio. Dottie looked as beautiful as ever and didn't want Dolly or anyone else to know she was still sick.

Video cameras recorded the studio events for inclusion in a documentary about Dottie's life, and producers would later interview Dolly about Gospel's sweetest songbird. As Dottie sat barefoot getting the last minute touches of her makeup, Dolly entered the room.

"Well," Dolly said with her trademark smile. "Who's having too much fun in here?"

"Hey baby," Dottie said as she hugged Dolly. "Well look at you and your cute little outfit."

While watching the Queen of Country Music and the Queen of Gospel Music recording musical history, I felt as if the rapture was taking place! What impressed me most was how Dolly looked after Dottie, taking her by the hand and constantly telling her how beautiful she looked and that she didn't look like she had been sick. With all her accomplishments, success and awards, Dolly could have easily came in with a diva attitude, but instead, I saw more *true* Christianity in her attitude than in most preachers we have met on the road.

The success of *Stand by the River* was more than we expected. Within two months of its release, the song found its way to the number one spot of the Christian Country music charts and countless American and European country music charts. It garnered nominations for two Christian Country Music Awards and a Dove Award, which is the highest achievement in Gospel music. The women would later win two Christian Fan Awards and I had the honor of presenting Dolly with one of hers for the duet that year.

With all the talk about

Dolly with Larry

Stand by the River at my home, my son, Christian, who was almost four at the time, developed a crush on Dolly.

"Daddy, I think we should buy Dolly one of GrandDot's guitars and send it to her for Christmas," he said in a pleading tone.

So for Christmas he and I sent Dolly a green heart-shaped *Dottie Rambo Kentuckian Guitar* and asked Dottie to write a little note on it. For the entire year of 2004, Dolly's *Chasing Rainbows Museum* in Dollywood displayed the guitar, all the awards the two had won for their duet, and the dress worn at the recording session.

Christian's crush grew and by his 5th birthday, he was able to see Dolly again in person. This was his big chance so he popped the question.

"Dolly, will you marry me?" he asked as romantically as a five-year-

55

Dolly and Christian share a personal moment together

old could muster.

"How about this," Dolly replied with a big smile. "When *I* grow up you and I can get married."

Christian beamed as Dolly signed a photograph for him and drew a heart on it. "I drew this heart on here so you can remember us getting married later!" Before Dolly left, she put Christian in her lap and snapped a picture.

Dottie was later invited to be the Gospel headliner for the opening of *Dollywood's Harvest Festival,* and the ladies would once again get to see each other.

"They don't have you outside in this heat, do they?" Dolly asked when she saw Dottie at the park.

"Oh no," Dottie replied. "I'm in a nice theater."

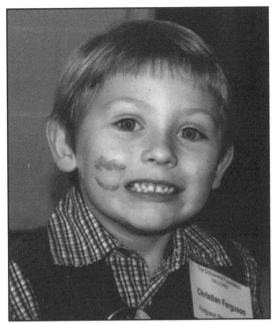

Christian shows off his kiss from Dolly

Dolly put her hands on her hips and winked. "I was going to say, they *better* take care of you down here."

As the two icons posed in a group photograph with all our crew and family, Dottie whispered, "Make sure to get a single with me and Dolly."

"We already had a single," Dolly said with a playful laugh. "It went number one and won a bunch of awards, where have you been?"

Then my star-struck son, Christian, asked Dolly for a kiss. She bent down to him and said, "Why don't *you* kiss *me* so I don't mess up my lipstick for the rest of the photos I have to do. Then when I'm done with all of this, I will come back and kiss *you*."

Of course, Christian was more than happy to kiss his first love as Dottie and I left to get ready for Dottie's next show. Judy, Christian and our little newborn son, Pierce, stayed behind, watching Dolly finish her photo session. Christian said good-bye when Dolly started to leave. "Oh Christian, I almost forgot your kiss," Dolly said, rushing back to him. A huge lipstick imprint was left on his cheek and he was one proud little boy!

Christian couldn't wait to get back to GranDot's dressing room to show off the lipstick on his cheek from his new girlfriend. My wife, Judy, couldn't wait to get there either: she wanted to let me know how much trouble I was in for leaving with our camera, causing her to miss some great shots with Dolly.

Dottie later called Christian onstage during her program so he could sing Dolly's part on *Stand by the River*. And, of course, he had to show off his lipstick imprint. Never one to be outdone, Dottie bent down and planted a big lipstick kiss on his other cheek. Christian would later ask me if he could leave the kisses on his cheeks without ever washing his face again. Laughing hysterically, I made an impression of the lip marks on a napkin and had them framed for him.

Gospel music couldn't ask for a better friend than Dolly Parton. Not only has she written some of the most beautiful Gospel songs, she has also shown support for the Gospel music industry. When the *Southern Gospel Music Association* was searching for a home for the *Hall Of Fame* and museum, Dolly came to the rescue, offering Dollywood as its home.

Dollywood's *Southern Gospel Jubilee* is one of the largest Gospel music festivals in the country, and the park even hosts a full-time Southern Gospel quartet, exposing millions of visitors a year to our music and heritage.

Dolly will always have a special place in my heart for being so gracious to an adoring little boy, and for showing such warmth and love to a woman who is like a mother to me. Dolly's kindness to me and my family will never be forgotten.

To borrow a line from one of her biggest songs: "Dolly Parton, I will always love you!"

Chapter 10
National Quartet Convention

My family and I love Dottie Rambo, and she has also meant a great deal to the National Quartet Convention. She is a true Gospel music legend.

—Claude Hopper

The *National Quartet Convention* is the largest annual gathering of fans and artists in Southern Gospel music. Fans from all over the world plan their vacations and holidays so they are able to enjoy the weeklong festivities and performances of their favorite artists. The convention first found its home in Memphis and Nashville, Tennessee before settling in Louisville, Kentucky, where it has remained since 1994.

I have never missed a convention while working with Dottie and have witnessed many memorable moments. My last memory of Hovie Lister was of him preaching from the convention stage. I remember George Younce and Jake Hess debuting the *Old Friends Quartet* on the same stage and thinking how history was in the making right before my eyes.

When Dottie enters the grounds of the NQC, it is as if Elvis has entered the building. When Dottie is on the schedule to sign autographs, a line will form as soon as officials open the doors to the public. Fans will wait for hours just to get a handshake, autograph, or photo with our little angel.

Despite her physical condition, Dottie is the most gracious artist I have ever seen with her fans. Not only will she sign whatever the fans bring her, she will sign as many items as they put before her and never complain. She will smile as many times as their camera will flash and make more personal time with each person than her body will allow.

I believe Dottie's enormous regard for her fans is why they love her so much. Dottie's favorite mantra to newer artists is *Untouchable, Unusable!* She elaborates: "The fans put me where I am today. They shared my music around the world. They bought my buses, bought my clothes, food and homes when buying my music. If you love them they will continue to love you."

I stand amazed at the many stories fans tell how Dottie has touched their lives in some way. One fan told me the story of hitchhiking to hear Dottie sing one night. The fan recalled meeting Dottie during the intermission and sharing the hitchhiking adventures with her. When Dottie returned to the stage, she asked someone to volunteer to take the fan safely back home.

Another fan shared how he saw a twelve-year-old Dottie Luttrell (Dottie's birth name) in a service and had followed her career since. Another fan shared how she met Dottie and another Gospel singer at the same time. The fan explained how the other singer ignored her while Dottie took the time to embrace her. Every fan has a story of a special moment with Dottie. Some may have never met Dottie, yet a song spoke to them at a friend or family member's funeral or wedding. All the same, Dottie listens to every story with genuine interest.

With as many heart-touching fan moments, there are just as many funny bone-tickling ones. One particular fan told Dottie, "I remember when you were a member of the Blackwood Brothers!"

"Honey," Dottie said with a chuckle. "I was never a Blackwood Brother."

Another woman approached Dottie and said, "I remember the first time I saw you. I still have that picture in my head. I even know what color dress you had on."

"Oh my goodness," Dottie said. "Well what color dress was it?"

Larry Ferguson, Dottie and Chris Barnes in the studio

The woman gave Dottie a deer-in-the-headlights look before saying, "Ah, I forgot."

"Well, do you remember what I was singing?" Dottie said smiling, trying to smooth over the poor woman's embarrassment.

"Yes, I do," the woman said with a reaffirmed smile. "I sure do."

"What was it?"

The woman's smile stretched further across her face. *"I Wouldn't Take Nothing for My Journey Now,"* she said boldly.

"That was Vestal Goodman, honey," Dottie said, finally giving up.

You meet all kinds. I remember an elderly fan came to our booth and started chatting. She told me how much Dottie had blessed her life and how she always bought everything that Dottie released. She then told me about the one Dottie Rambo project she found disappointing.

"I was so excited when Paul Crouch announced on TBN that they were making a movie about Dottie's life," the woman said. "I waited for the longest time and I just knew the movie had to be on video by now. So I sent my daughter to the video store with instructions to get the movie about Dottie Rambo. She brought it home and it was the awfulest thing I have ever watched!" By this time, the woman had her eyes closed and shaking her head. "It was full of war and shooting and it had Rocky in it. It wasn't like those Gaither videos."

Obviously, this poor woman's daughter had rented a *Rambo* action movie starring Sylvester Stallone. I couldn't get this poor dear to understand that TBN hadn't made the movie about Dottie's life yet.

Rarely, you can have an obtrusive person who just wants to cause a scene. In particular, one woman stood in Dottie's line for over two hours just to degrade her.

"When are you going to get your soul right?" she asked with a holier-than-thou tone.

"What do you mean?" Dottie said

Larry and his sons, Christian and Pierce, while off the road

with a sweet laugh. "My soul is just fine."

"No, you don't have your soul right because you left my denomination," the woman said. "You used to be holy and carry a license to preach from my organization!"

"No, honey," Dottie said. "I never belonged to your organization and never carried a license to preach through it. I am a little Bapticostal girl. I do love the people in your organization and have many friends in it, but I never belonged to any organization."

"You have just turned into a Jezebel and I *know* your soul is in danger," the woman said.

I happened to hear the woman's last statement and was ready to explode. As I stepped forward to tell her to take her tackiness elsewhere, Dottie stuck her hand up to let me know she would handle this spirit.

"Ma'am," Dottie said in a firm tone. "Just because you have never had a dab of cold cream on your face doesn't mean your soul is right." Dottie shared with her the Scriptures and the plan of salvation before explaining how we all served a merciful God—and it isn't about a particular card we carry, or the denomination we attend.

"You know I never thought about that before," the woman said. "I need to have my pastor invite you to come to our church." The woman then asked Dottie to sign a photo. Most people would have probably told this woman to take her picture and leave, but Dottie Rambo isn't most people.

For the most part, I am always with Dottie and can help her as she wades through the sea of people that surround her. After hours of signing at the NQC one night, Dottie realized she had to go to the little girl's room. There wasn't a private bathroom nearby and she assured me if we didn't get somewhere quick she would bring new meaning to *Shall We Gather at the River*.

We quickly found a public ladies room and I let Dottie know she was on her own from that point. While in her restroom stall, Dottie saw a hand protruding underneath the stall door. "Dottie would you sign my photo?" the voice of the fan said from the other side of the door.

"Not right now, honey," Dottie said. "I'm a little busy!"

Dottie's not the only victim of a confused fan at NQC. I fell prey to an avid Jonathon Martin fan attending the convention one year. According to some folks, I have a few facial features that vaguely resemble Jonathon Martin of the Southern Gospel trio The Martins. Therefore, fans have mistaken me for Jonathon Martin and even asked for an autograph in the past.

One night while walking in the NQC parking lot to pick up Dottie at her hotel, I felt an excruciating pain on the back of my head and I began falling backwards. I quickly caught my balance but my head felt like it was burning! As I rubbed the back of my hair, an enormous woman was running across the parking lot screaming, "I got a lock of Jonathon Martin's hair!"

Not only did I lose a great deal of hair, I had a huge scratch on my neck as well! This shook me up emotionally and angered me at the same time. You would think that no one would ever attempt bodily harm in order to get a souvenir from a Gospel artist. I went back to the hotel worried over a possible bald spot. Thank God I didn't have one. I called to let our booth workers know what was going on.

My best friend, Chris Barnes, was working at our booth that night and alerted NQC security. This was a smart move in case the real Jonathon Martin was to come face-to-face with this crazed fan. When I did come back to the exhibit hall, I heard all kinds of rumors. Nearly everyone I knew came by to check on me. Some heard rumors that someone robbed me and left me black and blue. One of the most absurd rumors was that Dottie and I arrived at the NQC in a limo, and someone stole Dottie's mink coat at gunpoint.

Toward the end of the night, I saw this big smile coming from around the corner—it was Jonathon Martin. He and his wife came by to check on me (no telling what rumors they had heard). He and I shared a laugh about my hair incident and the fact that Jonathon had recently shaved his head *bald!*

Chapter 11
Big Sister, Vestal Goodman

So, without planning on it, I said my good-bye to Vestal with the Homecoming gang the same way I met her: through a song.

—Larry Ferguson

All music genres have certain individuals who stand out more so than their peers. A God-given talent is what enables *the chosen* to touch more lives than the average artist. Unlike other genres, Gospel music doesn't have superstar figures in great numbers. As presenters of the Gospel, the artists seek to glorify God and to reach the lost and hurting.

It is uncommon for a Gospel artist to penetrate all genres of music, touching the lives of people outside the church walls and becoming what the world sees as a superstar. Perhaps only two individuals in our industry are what the world would label a superstar—and those two women happen to be *Dottie Rambo* and *Vestal Goodman*.

I can't think of any other artist in the Southern Gospel field who is equally famous outside the walls of our genre. Since the Gaither television and video series, many Southern Gospel artists are getting more exposure than ever before, but none has achieved the fame these women have reached. This is for many reasons—one being that they are two of the first female artists who broke into a male-dominated art form. In an era (and industry) of all-male quartets, both of these pioneers opened the doors for every female Gospel singer on the road today. These women also opened the doors for both men

Vestal Goodman with Larry

Larry and the always beautiful Dottie Rambo

Joan Rivers and Larry meet in New York

Larry's mother, Jackie, doesn't mind sharing her son with the Queen of Gospel music.

Reba Rambo McGuire, Dottie's daughter, poses with Larry

Stella Parton with Larry

LeAnn Rimes and Larry

Dolly Parton and Larry joke around

Every man's dream: a kiss from Dolly Parton

Reba Rambo McGuire on her 25th wedding anniversary

6

Larry and Dottie with longtime friend, Jim Bakker

Lily Tomlin at Larry and Judy's home

Judy, Keith Urban, Larry and his mom, Jackie, holding Christian

Having fun during a recent Kentucky M usic Hall of Fame award ceremony, Dottie, Lily Tomlin and Larry clown around for the camera

In 2006, Larry was honored to spend time with President Jimmy Carter joined by his wife, Rosalynn Carter

Has Dottie gone a bit overboard as she styles Larry's hair?

The great George Jones, one of Dottie's favorite Country singers

Christian and Lily Tomlin

Dottie is an accomplished guitarist

Dolly with Christian Ferguson

11

Pierce, Shayde (Dottie's beloved pet), Dottie and Christian on the bus

Like mother and son, Larry and Dottie have a special bond

Judy, Dottie, Tammy Faye, Larry and Christian join together for a photo shoot

12

Lily and Larry join Dottie as she is inducted into the
Kentucky Music Hall of Fame; below, the Ferguson family

13

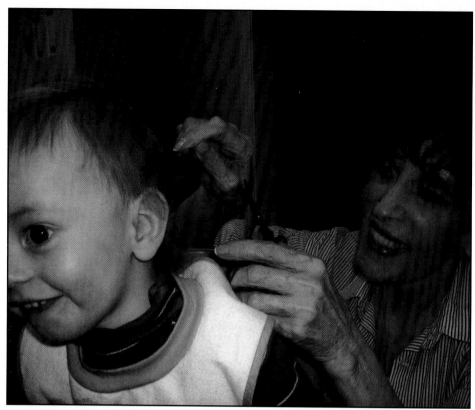

Pierce gets his first haircut, and is GranDot getting scissor-happy?

Dottie's Grandchildren, Destiny and Israel, pose with GranDot, Dottie's daughter, Reba, and Larry as they visit Dottie on Christmas.

Uh, is someone addicted to candy? You decide!

On the Skylift at Gatlinburg; below, Carol Channing

To my dear friend Larry with such Happy memories.
Carol Channing

and women with a more ministry-minded, yet entertainment-based, career.

They shared the same success of quickly crossing over into a country sound when most Gospel recordings leaned heavily on piano and shape-note singing. This music touched the hearts and lives of many people and many classes. Not only did society's higher echelon take notice, but so did the hardworking farmer and mountain preachers.

What I find more amazing about these women is that even though their successes ran neck-to-neck in the competitive world of music, they were best friends. Known to each other as big sister (Vestal) and little sister (Dottie), they carried a bond that carried far beyond the walls of musical pals. If one found herself in trouble, the other would be there in an instant. More times than I can remember, Dottie has told me she couldn't have been any closer to Vestal if she had been her own blood sister.

The first time I witnessed the impact these women had on the public was at the *National Quartet Convention*. Vestal and Howard had re-formed The Happy Goodmans as a trio with Johnny Minick and traveled as part of the Gaither concert tour. Because of extensive touring schedules on both sides, the women hadn't seen each other in some time. Vestal's son, Rick, sent for Dottie to come see Howard and Vestal at their booth. As these two women embraced, cameras flashed so fast it looked like we were in the middle of an electrical storm.

On another occasion, we were at an event with the Goodmans and Vestal recognized a person there who in the past had taken advantage of Dottie financially and hurt her deeply. Vestal charged toward me like a general at war with her signature hanky in hand. She grabbed my forearms and glared deep into my eyes.

"Don't you let that person anywhere near Dottie!" she said, quickly letting me know who the boss was. She stood guard like a hawk, making sure Dottie had protection from this person. I knew then how much she loved Dottie and for that, I had the utmost respect for her.

Where Vestal exuded boldness, Howard was more of a gentle natured person in the times I was around him. Nearly every time he saw Dottie, he would give her a childlike grin while tugging at the waist of his slacks and say, "Dottie, just look at how much weight I've lost!"

While filming Gaither's *Heaven* video, I remember Howard telling Dottie about his new workout regiment. "They have me doing a little of this and a little of that," he said, detailing his workout sessions.

"That's great Howard," Dottie said. "Don't you feel better after doing that?"

"NO!" Howard said with a laugh. "I can't tell it's doing me any good and I hurt worse!"

Dottie and Vestal sat close to each other during the filming at that same event while the young group performing in the final segment had to do a few retakes—Dottie all the while needing to go to the restroom. Knowing the camera could be on her at any time, Dottie tried to ignore the call of nature. She finally leaned over to Vestal, explained her predicament, and asked what she should do.

"Oh honey, come on and I'll take you," Vestal said. "If these kids ain't got it right by now, we're liable to be here all night!" As one onlooker gave Vestal a curious look, she looked them right in the eye while walking past. "Everybody's gotta go sometime," she said, waving her hanky like a flag while Dottie laughed all the way to the little girl's room.

Howard sure lived up to his nickname, Happy. He was the jolliest, friendliest person you could ever meet. I remember one concert at which Vestal announced that she had a new *Vestal and Friends* CD coming out and named many country artists who would be performing duets with her. Howard quickly interrupted Vestal's advertisement with a question: "I want to know when you are going to do something with Dolly Parton?" he said.

Vestal gave him a schoolmarm glare and said, "Why do *you* want to know?"

"Look," Howard said with a laugh. "I may have bad knees but there isn't a thing wrong with my eyes!" The audience roared with laughter.

Sadly, we lost Howard in November of 2002, and it was a difficult time for Gospel music. The Happy Goodmans would now live only in our memories. Everyone wondered how Vestal would continue without her faithful helpmate, but true to her calling, Vestal never missed a step and went right back to the ministry.

The most precious memory I have of Vestal is of her in a rehearsal hall before a television special that included both women. Vestal's rehearsal was running close to Dottie's timeslot so we sat and listened as Vestal belted out her tunes as only Vestal could. When finished, she ran over to Dottie and sat chatting for some time. As Vestal started to leave, she walked over to me and said, "God called you to take care of her," she said, pointing toward Dottie. She then began praying and prophesying over me. Nearly everything she spoke over me has already come to pass. No picture, autograph or souvenir could ever measure up to a moment like that.

Late one rainy night traveling from Louisville to Nashville, I received a call from Dottie's daughter, Reba. I knew something was wrong because

Larry with Big Sister and Little Sister

it was an odd time of night for Reba to be calling.

"Are you with Mother?" Reba asked.

I told her no, that I was on my way home from visiting relatives in Louisville.

"Well, have you heard?" Reba said in a grave tone.

"No, what?"

Reba sounded as though she was trying to regain composure. "A friend of Vestal's granddaughter, Leslie, just called telling us that Vestal passed away a few hours ago."

To be honest, as I drove down I-65 South, I couldn't comprehend what Reba was telling me. Vestal Goodman—this powerhouse of a woman with more boldness and strength than anyone I had ever met—was gone just like that?

"Oh my goodness," I said to Reba. "This is going to devastate Dottie."

"I don't know what to do," Reba said. "I'm going to call her right now and tell her. I just wish you were in town so you could be there with her when I give her the news." Reba paused a second to steady her voice. "I know if I wait, someone will call and spring the news on her, making it worse."

We ended our conversation and within minutes, I received a call from Dottie.

"Larry," she said, crying, "I lost my big sissy."

Words can never comfort a person in a situation like that. Decades of friendship and the end of an era had taken place. A simple *I'm sorry* just couldn't comfort Dottie at that point. As long as I have known her, this was the hardest death I have ever seen Dottie deal with.

Leading up to Vestal's funeral, Dottie's spiritual strength would rise up and she wanted to be as much comfort to Vestal's son, Rick, as possible. Rick has taken flack over the years for being protective of his parents and especially of Vestal. What people don't realize is that Rick and his wife, Diane, had a call on their lives to guard and protect the gift within his parents. My wife and I have the same call on our lives with Dottie, so we understand the sacrifices his family made to present the Gospel through his parents. Dottie knew that she had to endure her own physical and emotional pain to be at Vestal's funeral for Rick—and for herself.

Bill Gaither planned a special Homecoming tribute to Vestal with the choir singing all the songs that this *superstar* made popular. Rick entered the rehearsal handing out Vestal's white hankies to all the women in the choir.

As we left the rehearsal room, Rick took us to a private area for Dottie to say good-bye to Vestal one last time. Vestal's family and a few special friends (Michael W. Smith, Amy Grant and Vince Gill) were all there paying their respects. Dottie looked up, fighting back her tears and said, "Well, she and Howard are together now kicking up gold dust!"

"That's right, Dottie," Amy Grant said with a huge smile. "They sure are!"

Dottie took her place in the Homecoming Choir and I started toward the sanctuary auditorium. "You can't leave me," Dottie said, grabbing my arm.

"Dottie, this is for the Homecoming singers and I don't think Bill would want me up here," I said. "I would look out of place."

"Look, you're with me and I need you," Dottie said. "They'll understand."

So, without planning on it, I said my good-bye to Vestal with the Homecoming gang the same way I met her: through a song.

Chapter 12
What's Up, Doc?

Well, I still did good, broken tooth and all, didn't I?

—Loretta Lynn

A smile is one of the most important assets a singer has. Think about it: who in their right mind wants to see a celebrity with decaying teeth? Appearance—*even in the Gospel music industry*—is almost as important as the artist's talent.

Our former dentist, the late James McPherson, was one of the greatest smile-providers in the country. Not only was he one of the jolliest men in the world, he was also one of the kindest and gentlest. He is responsible for many famous smiles: Ms. Dottie, Loretta Lynn, Randy Travis, the late Vestal Goodman and many of the Nashville Titans football players.

Dr. McPherson passed away a few years ago but left us with some wonderful memories. He loved showing off his celebrity clientele. If you were a celebrity in his dental chair, it wasn't uncommon for him to bring someone over for a quick meet-and-greet. He loved spending quality time with his well-known patients, asking questions and teasing.

And his celebrity patients loved spending quality time with him— even while sitting in a dentist chair! Because of these relationships, Dr. McPherson had received some wonderful celebrity memorabilia over the years.

While visiting for a checkup one day, I noticed a framed bottle of superglue among the items decorating his wall. "Why do you have this?" I asked, pointing to the odd item.

"Oh, *that*," he said with a chuckle. "Well, Loretta Lynn was doing a show at her ranch in Hurricane Mills and broke a cap on a tooth." He paused a second, trying to keep a straight face. "I couldn't get to her before the show so she superglued it! I could have died!" By this time, he could no longer hold back the grin. "So, as a joke, Loretta had *this* framed for me." He pointed to a handwritten note from the country singer.

"Doc, you are not going to believe this," I said, laughing. "I was at that show! Loretta told the audience about gluing the tooth and I have pictures of her pointing to it while onstage!"

Dr. McPherson's staff scheduled Dottie and Loretta to be in the office

A beautiful smile

at the same time for our next visit. Dottie was already in the chair for routine cleaning when in walks the Coal Miner's Daughter. Dr. McPherson told me to be watching for a special person walking past, but I had no idea who it would be.

Not a minute later, Dr. McPherson motioned for me to come with him. "Dottie's in a chair in one room and Loretta's in a chair in another," he said. "There is no way I am going to let either of them see each other like that, but I want you to come back and meet Loretta."

"Loretta, I want you to meet one of my patients," Dr. McPherson said. "He was at the concert where you superglued that tooth back on."

"Ah, you were," Loretta said with a playful grin. "Well, I still did good, broken tooth and all, didn't I?"

"You were great," I said. "I snapped some photos of you playing with the tooth that night."

"Oh no, well you need to let him see them," Loretta said, pointing to Dr. McPherson. "No, don't do that, he'll hang them on the wall!"

After a short chat with Loretta, I made my way back to Dottie and noticed one of the Titans football players coming in. A few minutes later country singer Linda Davis walked in.

A red-faced Dr. McPherson came over to finish his work on Dottie and said, "Dottie, I'm going to fix you up, girl." He then looked at me and said. "I'm going to kill my staff for doing this to me. They have Dottie and Loretta here at the same time and Linda Davis, and one of the Titans football players, and Vestal Goodman is on her way. I can't spend any time with them like this!"

The good doctor was also *my* dentist and gave me the smile I have today. Once, after some dental surgery in his office, my wife, Judy, and her sister, Becky, picked me up. As they waited for me in the waiting room, in walks Loretta Lynn.

Becky nudged Judy and said, "Oh my gosh, that's Loretta Lynn!" This made Becky's day as she was only visiting for the weekend and now could go back home with a great story.

Judy and Becky had to help me walk out of the building because I was still woozy from the medicine used during my surgery.

As we walked through the hall, the technicians walked me past Loretta's chair and said, "Larry, say hello to Loretta Lynn."

"Oh good grief, she must live here," the medicine said for me. "She seems to be here every time I'm here!"

Each visit after this embarrassing moment, Dr. McPherson never missed a chance to tease me about my experience. He finally assured me that Loretta was under medication as well, and she wouldn't remember it either.

Loretta Lynn

Photos from here and there

Willie Nelson, Larry and Christian

Bonnie Raitt

Larry, Pierce and Dottie at dinner

Larry, Barbara Fairchild and Dottie

A great pose

Dolly Parton

Bill Gaither and Larry during a Gaither Homecoming concert

Karen Peck Gooch

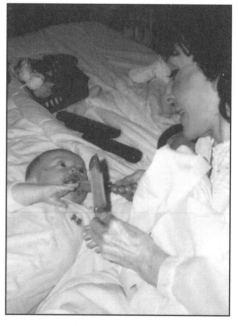

Dottie feeds Pierce fudgecicles

Thanksgiving 2005 at Dottie's home in Nashville

Judy, Brad Paisley, and Larry meet behind stage

Larry, Shayde, Judy, Pierce, Dottie, Chris Barnes and Christian

The hilarious Aaron Wilburn shares some of his comedy on stage with Larry—bless his heart

Pierce attempts to brush Dad's teeth before a concert date

Larry with the great Carl Perkins

Judy and Larry pose with the incomparable Charlie Daniels

Brenda Lee poses for the camera

Larry and Dottie inside the tour bus

77

Larry and Dottie clown around shortly after her leg break and recovery process

Dottie with Dean Hopper, of the Hoppers

Dottie, Larry and Bill Anderson

Larry, Dottie and Louise Mandrell in Pigeon Forge

Spending time with Pat Boone

Dottie greets Jim Ed Brown with a kiss

Larry and Dottie with Grand Ole Opry member John Conlee

Sharon White, Larry, Connie Smith and Barbara Fairchild

Jan Crouch, Dottie and Larry pose after a taping at TBN

Chapter 13
Barbara Mandrell, Larry Gatlin and a Star-Studded Tribute

God blessed my dear friend, Dottie Rambo, by putting Larry Ferguson into her life.

—Barbara Mandrell

After the success of A&E's *Biography*, CMT's *The Life and Times* and VH1's *Behind The Music*, The *Total Living Network* (TLN) collaborated with *Stephen Yake Productions* to produce a biographical series on Gospel Music legends.

Both companies found success in the Christian entertainment field, with dozens of programming specials airing on major cable and network stations. Stephen Yake directed all the videos for contemporary Christian artist Carman, pioneering the music concept video in the Christian industry. TLN's Jerry Rose was one of the most respected leaders in Christian television.

Work began on the series, including episodes on Ms. Dottie, The Happy Goodmans, The Blackwoods and so many others. The name of the series, *More Than The Music*, fittingly described the message of hope and grace that these artists had traveled the world proclaiming.

Not long after the project had started, the producer, Cindy Montano, called my office requesting photos and archival footage for Dottie's episode. Cindy invited me to the production office, where we discussed the program in length. Little did I know our visit would end up birthing a new project for Dottie.

"I've always wanted to produce a television program where country music artists paid tribute to Dottie," I said. "The artists could share stories about Dottie and perform her songs."

TBN had produced a wonderful tribute to Dottie several years earlier but mainly focused on Christian artists. I wanted a program featuring celebrities from outside the Christian music genre, focusing solely on country music artists.

"WOW, what an idea!" Cindy said. "You know, the place to have a

Dottie and Larry meet with dear friend, Barbara Mandrell

special like that would be the Ryman Auditorium. Its history with all-night Gospel sings and The Grand Ole Opry makes it an ideal location."

By the end of the visit, we pitched the idea to financiers from TLN, who happened to be meeting upstairs. And by the end of the month, we had a budget and time frame set. The only change to our original plans was that the artist lineup included non-country artists as well. TLN felt we should feature Gospel artists alongside country performers, featuring Southern and traditional Black Gospel. I still hope someday to get a country music tribute to Dottie made in audio form, but I was happy with TLN's decision.

As we began working on the project, I was to book all the artists for the program and its host. The key to every good television special is someone who can make everything come together.

We needed a host from outside the normal walls of Gospel music with the ability to attract a wider television audience. This person would also need the skills and showmanship to host a live program, where twists, turns, and off-the-cuff humor are always certain.

Everyone involved in the project had a wish list. Jerry Rose suggested Dolly Parton, but I didn't want to keep asking favors of Dolly when she had already been so gracious with her time. She had recently agreed to perform a duet on Dottie's album and had agreed to an interview about Dottie for the *More Than The Music* episode. I *did* compromise by asking

Stars gather together for the Dottie Rambo Tribute project

Dolly if we could shoot a music video for the special on the day she gave the interview for Dottie's life story episode. Dolly, being as generous with her valuable time as she is, did agree and although we didn't have her as a host, we *did* have her presence in the special.

Several other suggestions came to the table but none seemed right for the show we were doing. The first person that came to my mind was Barbara Mandrell. You couldn't ask for a more seasoned television personality. She has proven herself as a live performer who could easily pick up any mistakes or unscripted banter during a show of this nature.

With her keen stage presence, Barbara had proven she was more than capable of bringing in a television viewing audience. After all, she starred in one of the most successful television variety series on NBC during the 80's. More important, Barbara had a history with Dottie. A host of a Dottie Rambo tribute should not only have knowledge of her vast body of work, but should also know Dottie's heart and love her as a person. Barbara fit this description better than anyone else in the business.

Barbara's history with Dottie dates back over two decades. When Barbara recorded her Grammy winning project *He Set My Life To Music*, she called on many Christian artists for help, including Dottie. The pair recorded a duet on what would become one of Dottie's most popular songs, *I Will Glory In The Cross*. Barbara also filmed two shows with Dottie for her *Dottie Rambo Magazine* television series.

Apart from work, the two women spent a lot of time together visiting at shows, attending church or just having lunch. I couldn't imagine anyone else hosting this special.

Barbara had officially retired from the music business and was currently only accepting acting roles. Although she could still host the show without singing, we didn't know if she would be willing to do so. After all this consideration, I just assumed that Barbara would be an unattainable goal. Trying to avoid disappointment, I chose not to shoot for something I was more than likely going to miss. Therefore, I decided to put off asking Barbara.

Not wanting to settle for just any host, however, I decided to get Dottie's opinion. I explained how well everything was going with the special but we still needed a host. I then asked her to go over her vast number of friends for the best-suited person.

Without hesitation, Dottie said, "Well, you know Barbara Mandrell would be perfect."

Now with both of us feeling strongly about Barbara, I had to explain to Dottie that Barbara had retired from singing and may not want to be a part of a musical special.

"Retired?" Dottie said with a laugh. "Larry, she's too *young* to retire!"

I explained that Barbara now focused on acting roles and no longer performed in musical events. I told her we couldn't be certain that she would even consider hosting the special.

"Would you like me to call and ask her?" Dottie said.

Who could turn down such an offer? Within the hour, Dottie would either solve my hosting problem or tell me to start looking elsewhere. Dottie called and Barbara accepted. It was then I knew we were going to have a special production ahead of us.

With Dolly's video duet with Dottie, and now Barbara Mandrell hosting, our show was off to a great start. I then contacted Larry Gatlin's office and within the week, I received a call from Larry himself telling me he would love to be on the program. "I'll jump at any excuse to love on Dottie," he said with a laugh.

We then secured country stars Crystal Gayle, Barbara Fairchild and Stella Parton. We added Gospel legends Vestal Goodman, The Speer Family, the Jordonaires, Albertina Walker and Jessy Dixon. And to give the new sound of Southern Gospel music a voice, we added The Crabb Family and Dottie's favorite of the newer groups: the Isaacs.

After each artist chose a Dottie Rambo song to perform, it seemed everything was moving along smoothly. In our production meeting, someone suggested we add a family moment by having Reba perform a duet with her mother. I mentioned we should also include Dottie's granddaughter, Destiny, which would make a great moment in television history and the family as three generations of Rambo women shared the stage in song. The trio had never performed onstage together (and have not since the filming) so this would be the rare and special moment our production team wanted. Not to mention Dottie could give a platform to her granddaughter that she had never had at that point.

July 31, 2002, will always be a special day for me. I felt like a father expecting a child's birth. Our dream of this particular project had finally come to life. As we rolled into the Ryman Auditorium alley, I remember praying and hoping this would be a night Dottie would be proud of. If she wasn't happy with the evening then all the work was in vain. This was her night and I wanted her to know that.

As she got out of her car and made her way to the Ryman stage door, Dottie graciously signed autographs for fans that had waited in the alley. This is a Nashville tradition for fans. There is only one artist entrance into the building so whenever your favorite artist performs there, you know you will have a chance to meet them in the alley. That is, unless they're too snooty to stop! Dottie is not one of those artists who turn fans away, so after signing and taking photos, security guards urged her inside where Larry Gatlin waited with open arms!

I can't tell you what it was like to see those two together. Larry is such a jokester and as he hugged and doted on Dottie, I could tell he was sincere. It was obvious he respected this godly woman and felt a deep affection for her. Whether it was a songwriting connection, singing connection or just plain friendship, you knew these two had a spiritual bond.

Shortly before the stage call, a knock came on Dottie's dressing room door and as I answered, standing before me was Barbara Mandrell, dressed in all white with the deepest blue eyes you could ever imagine— a beauty to behold. As she walked into the room, she and Dottie were like two girls at their high school reunion. It was a moment I will never forget. As the two caught up and shared how special it was to be with each other again, I was as proud as a peacock for Dottie and thanked God for bringing this together.

Barbara laid a hand on Dottie's knee and said, "Do you mind if I have prayer with you before we start the show?"

"Would I mind?" Dottie laughed. "I would love it!"

Barbara took Dottie by the hand and prayed one of the sweetest prayers my ears have ever heard. As she prayed, one of the production assistants kept telling me we were running a few minutes late and I needed to interrupt them.

"There is no way I am going to tell Barbara Mandrell to stop her prayer and jump out onstage," I said to the man.

"Well then," he said with a red face. "I guess we'll have to start the show without them!"

I looked him in the eye and laughed. Did this guy really believe he could start a show without its host or its star? If so, he was a novice at his trade. In all fairness, he was merely doing his job and probably getting flack from someone higher up in production. But if he could pull off his threat, he was a real miracle worker.

Barbara graced the Ryman stage to a wonderful ovation, and as host, she never faltered. She spoke every word with poise and the audience followed her every graceful move. Barbara wore a ring Dottie had given her years ago. Known as the *Rambo Ring*, its design was of a ram holding a bow in its mouth. This served as the logo for many of Dottie's businesses in her early days and Barbara had kept it all these years. Barbara's heart for her friend moved me...and it moved the entire audience as well.

Crystal Gayle

A tearful moment took place when Crystal Gayle, in all her elegance, graced the stage to sing one of my favorite Dottie compositions, *Tiny*.

Dottie wrote the song for a young fan named Jennifer Meade, who was eight-years-old and dying of leukemia. The little girl loved Dottie so much that she always wanted to dress and sing like her. Jennifer passed away shortly after Dottie wrote the song, but her mother, Donna, sat in the audience at the Ryman Auditorium and listened as Crystal shared their story before singing the song. Many people have said that was one of the most moving moments in the show. After Crystal finished, Barbara asked Donna to stand and we felt it was a great tribute to the song, the Lord and little Jennifer.

When Vestal Goodman claimed the stage, it was only fitting she sing the song that launched Dottie's songwriting career: *There's Nothing My God Can't Do.* Vestal had the first recording of that song, and after hearing Vestal sing it, Governor Jimmie Davis signed Dottie to her first song-writer's contract in the 60's. Later in the show, Vestal and Dottie performed *Holy Spirit Thou Art Welcome In This Place,* and it was something watching these two Gospel icons singing live at the Ryman Auditorium. Little did we know this would be the last time the two would ever perform together.

As the show went on, Jessy Dixon brought everyone to their feet as he asked Dottie to join him on *I've Never Been This Homesick Before.* The crowd clapped and cheered as Vestal paced back-and-forth backstage wringing her hanky. Finally she raised both hands in the air and said to me, "Honey get me a microphone...I gotta go out there and sing with them!"

Vestal joined them onstage and it was all caught on tape. Between all the artists, we had a project that was sure to bless the hearts of many and paid tribute to a most deserving woman.

I was happy to be a co-creator and associate producer for a project praising Dottie and the God she served. I believe He was as happy with it as any of us were.

Chapter 14
Closed Minds

We judge this sad misfortune but rarely take the time
to reach out in sweet compassion, pouring the oil and
the wine.

—**Dottie Rambo,** *The Oil and the Wine*

"How dare you be seen in *that*!"

Those were the first words in an e-mail I received from a concert attendee in Cullman, Alabama. She didn't stop there.

"I came to see Dottie Rambo in concert and you, her manager, show up wearing a red shirt and tie under your jacket!"

At first, I thought the message was a practical joke. Surely no one would object to someone wearing a shirt and tie to a concert! As I continued reading, I realized I was correct; the shirt and tie were not what bothered her.

"Red is a sinful color," she continued in her message, "and a dear sweet anointed woman like Dottie Rambo should not have to associate with someone running around in red, promoting sin!"

Getting this far into the e-mail, I felt my face getting as red as the shirt and tie in question. According to this woman, when I wore the color red it somehow reduced Dottie's spirituality.

I normally delete messages like this, but I felt compelled to reply.

I explained to her that I did not intend to offend anyone with how I dress, and that I was sorry she had a problem with the color of my wardrobe. I also told her that I did not personally associate the color red with sin and pointed out that the color of the blood of Christ was red.

"In a faith where our whole salvation comes from the Blood of Christ," I wrote, "how could you possibly think it's the color of sin?"

I told her that if she could give me one Biblical or logical proof that wearing the color red promotes sin I would gladly purge my wardrobe of the color.

"By the way," I continued in my e-mail, "didn't you notice the solid red dress Dottie wore that night?"

I never heard back from the woman, but this is sadly a common case in Gospel music. Too many people will cast verbal stones without thinking of what they are saying.

I will never forget the wise words on this subject from Christian comedian Mark Lowry. He and Dottie were in concert together one night and Mark made some comments from the stage that hit home for me.

"Have you heard the old saying *hate the sin and love the sinner?*" Mark said from the stage. "Well, I've stopped doing that!"

An uncomfortable hush came over the crowd. "How could he stop doing that?" fans whispered to the person in the next seat. "What is he talking about?"

"It's time we hate *our own* sin and love the sinner!" Mark announced.

These words were powerful to me. Too many times people of the faith attack others yet never extend a hand of love or compassion. One of my favorite songs Dottie wrote is one that speaks of this issue: *The Oil and the Wine.* One line in the song says, "We judge this sad misfortune but rarely take the time to reach out in sweet compassion, pouring the oil and the wine."

After a concert one night at a rural church, a drunken man waited in Dottie's autograph line. The promoter of the event was a local pastor and knew the man was an alcoholic. "Get out of here right now and go home," the pastor told the man.

"I need to say something to Dottie," the man said with a thick tongue.

"You are not going to say anything to Dottie," the pastor said. "Now go home or I am going to have to make you leave."

"Is something wrong?" Dottie asked.

"Well, Ms. Dottie," the pastor said. "This gentleman shouldn't be here tonight."

A curious look came over Dottie's face. "Why not?"

"He has a problem," the pastor said.

Dottie put her hands on her hips and said, "Well that's why he *should*

Dottie sings on stage with Christian

be here!"

During another concert autograph session, a woman broke down into tears while speaking to Dottie.

"My son loves you so much," she said through sobs. "But he won't get in the line because he thinks you would look down on him."

"Why would he think that?" Dottie asked.

The woman leaned toward Dottie and said, "He has Aids."

"You tell him to come here right now."

The man approached the table with his head down and avoided Dottie's eyes.

"Son, why did you think I would look down on you?" Dottie said in a soft tone.

"I was told that God gave me this disease," he said, finally looking up. "And my church withdrew me from the congregation."

"Honey, God didn't give you this disease." Dottie then began ministering to this broken man.

As he started to leave, he turned to Dottie and asked if he could touch her hand. "You may be afraid to touch me," he said, "and if you are, I understand."

Dottie kissed him on the cheek and said, "I'm not afraid to touch you."

Chapter 15
Lockdown

About the time our plane landed, an unidentified man ran into the airport, threw a bag to the floor and yelled, "Bomb in the bag!"

—Larry Ferguson

Flying is as much a part of our travels as hotels and room service. Some trips are just unreasonable to drive; so like birds, we take to the skies.

One trip to Dallas, Texas, proved to be one flight we would just as soon forget...but never will.

When driving to concert dates, Dottie and I generally travel alone, but our webmaster, Chris, usually joins us when we fly. On this particular trip, we flew into Dallas, looking forward to a good night's rest before the next day's concert at Will Rogers Auditorium. However, our good night's rest turned into one of the craziest ordeals of our travels.

About the time our plane landed, an unidentified man ran into the airport, threw a bag to the floor and screamed, "BOMB IN THE BAG!"

After making this terrifying announcement, the man removed all his clothing and ran away naked! Now, I'm not sure if he thought he would be less noticeable running nude, or if he just didn't want to get his new clothes dirty if the bomb exploded. The whole nudity thing was as absurd to me as the bomb threat.

Authorities told us (and our waiting escorts) that the airport was in a *lockdown* state, meaning no one could leave the airport. A few moments later, another attendant came over and said, "Bomb sniffing dogs are acting as though the bag

During a flight

has a bomb in it."

"What?" Dottie said with wide eyes.

I could feel my face and neck growing warm with anger. "Well, if it is a bomb," I said, "does it make sense to keep us locked down where the bomb will kill us?"

"Well listen," Dottie said with rising boldness. "We are not just going to sit here and let some little man scare us. God is bigger than any bomb! Let's all join hands right here and pray!"

Dottie began praying and taking authority over the situation and we began calming down. My biggest concern was Dottie. She was still recovering from a broken femur and the many effects of a lifetime of back problems. I knew this was all taking a toll on her body and arranged for her to lie down in a private room. Therefore, I entrusted our escorts with Dottie while Chris and I waited out the lockdown.

By this time, more flights had arrived and within forty-five minutes, you could barely see the floor for all the people. An hour later, every restaurant ran out of food. Now you have a mixture of irritated, weary travelers who are also hungry and disgruntled.

Perhaps Chris enjoys being in a crisis with me because I usually make a fool out of myself. I figure if you have to pass the time, why not have some fun doing it. For instance, I overheard many people wondering why we had to wait so long in (what they perceived as) long lines.

I thought this was odd since the airport continually announced what was going on. Therefore, I started saying things to Chris loud enough for those around me to hear. "I'm glad we got in line early to get Oprah Winfrey's autograph," I said with a straight face. "I can't believe this many people would want her autograph!"

Within an hour or two, the airport began passing out free bags of peanuts and water to the delayed multitude. "Peanuts?" I said with a joke, "I want a free flight!" I probably shouldn't have mumbled this because a woman next to me began demanding a free flight, too.

After close to seven hours (although the news reported it as five), authorities finally allowed us to leave the airport.

"Well Chris," Dottie said as we made our way to the exit doors. "Did Larry get you into any trouble?"

"Oh yes," Chris replied, "as always!"

After getting into the car, Dottie said she'd heard that authorities took the naked man to a mental facility. "Honey, I'm ready to go to Heaven when God calls me," she said. "I'm ready to go up at any time, but I don't want to go up in pieces!"

Chapter 16
Jake Hess

Words cannot describe the class this man had.

—Larry Ferguson

I think it should be an unpardonable sin to look up the word *integrity* in the dictionary and not see a picture of the late Jake Hess next to the definition. Apart from being one of the most honored men in Gospel music, Jake was one of the most gentle and sincere. In the competitive world of Gospel music, Jake managed to become the most beloved, envied, and non-threatening person ever to pick up a microphone.

My first dealings with Jake came before I began working with Dottie. As a young concert promoter, I thought of Jake Hess as one of my dream concerts. I had tried for about three years to book him, but because of his health issues, it was almost impossible. I was finally able to get him booked, and the Gospel music lovers of Louisville welcomed him with a great deal of enthusiasm.

The day of the concert, Jake and his bus driver, Lightning, rolled onto the parking lot of the auditorium, where Jake invited me onboard. I felt like a child meeting Santa Claus for the first time. Jake traded in his famous toupee for a baseball cap, but his famous smile was still present.

"Where would you like to eat?" Jake asked to my surprise.

"Anywhere you would like to go is fine with me," I replied.

Lightning then said, "Let's go somewhere that has vegetables; the boss is a diabetic so we need to look out for him."

I quickly thought of the closest place in town with-

Dottie and Larry pose with the legendary Jake Hess

out realizing that it was the most popular senior citizen establishment for belly-pleasing grub. You can only imagine what it was like to walk in to a crowded senior hangout with Jake Hess.

As we ate, Jake asked how old I was. I told him reluctantly (which I will not do in this book—Ha-Ha). Embarrassed at my youth, I feared Jake would not take me seriously now. Jake quickly put me at ease.

"Never tell anyone your age," he told me. "The younger promoters are the best, but some people would hold your age against you. I've seen older promoters who couldn't pull off what you have."

I soaked up every word of advice from a legend who had seen more of the world in the early half of his life than I will in the entirety of mine. Jake went on to tell me of a teenager who once promoted the Statesmen. He said the boy was around fifteen years old and had called Hovie Lister, inquiring about booking them. Hovie treated the boy like any other promoter and gave him their standard fee. The young promoter asked if Hovie could work with him on the price and Lister sternly held his guns.

"Son, if you want to do this you gotta do it right," Hovie said, politely. "I'm willing to give you a chance but not a favor." Jake explained that this teenage promoter was one of the best they ever worked with. I felt encouraged by his story and always followed his advice. To this day, I have never revealed my age, although I now admit, the main reason is vanity. I wish I were still trying to *hide* the young part!

The concert was a huge success and I watched in amazement at how personable Jake was. I had never seen an artist, especially one of his stature, make himself as accessible as he did. As people came into the concert hall, Jake greeted them at one door shaking hands and thanking them for coming. Normally the headline artist will hide before the show and if you do see him or her for a meet-and-greet session, it is at the artist's merchandise table following the performance. Jake broke all stereotypes.

As the Journeymen performed their opening act, Jake sat in the audience, drinking in every song, and even invited the group to join him during his portion to sing old Statesmen tunes.

My wife and I had just received news that she was expecting our first child, Christian, and we hadn't formally made the announcement yet. Word got to Jake, and he not only announced it from the stage but also said he wanted to be the first to congratulate me. He went on to tell me his son, Jake, Jr., and daughter-in-law, Judy Martin, were having a baby or else Jake, Jr., would have accompanied him to the concert.

After the concert was over, I paid Jake and thanked him for the wonderful night. A few minutes after he left, I noticed he was back in the building and walking toward me.

"I wanted to let you know that I am going to tell Mary Ann (Mary Ann Addison was his booking agent) that I only want to work with you when coming to Louisville," he said, shaking my hand.

A few days after the concert, the phone rang and it was Jake.

"Larry, I just wanted to call and make sure everything went all right," Jake said, "and to see if you were happy with everything."

Words cannot describe the class this man had.

From the night of the concert on, most of my dealings with Jake would be meetings at Gaither events that I worked with Dottie. Dottie adored Jake and called him *Mr. Integrity*. In the 1960s, Dottie recorded an album with Jake Hess and The Imperials. In fact, Jake brought Dottie's group, The Gospel Echoes, to Warner Brothers' attention.

One particular Gaither concert in Nashville, Bill had called on Dottie to sing *Too Much to Gain to Lose*. Dottie was aware that Jake had just recorded and released the song on his latest album and suggested in front of the live audience that Jake do it as "nobody can sing it like him."

"Honey, there is no way I could sing that song sitting on the stage with you," Jake said. Dottie obliged Bill and the crowd with her rendition.

The last time I spoke to Jake was by telephone. While sitting in my office, I received a call from *Mr. Gospel Music*. "Larry, I wanted to call because I heard Dottie is bad off in the hospital," he said with compassion.

"No, she is doing just fine," I said. "I just saw her a few minutes ago."

"Well, that is why I called to check," Jake said with a laugh. "You know, the rumors had me dead before!"

To me, Jake Hess's death was probably one of the greatest losses Gospel music ever suffered. Our younger artists have lost one of the greatest mentors. Songs have suffered the loss of the greatest Gospel male vocalist, and fans have lost a legend.

Chapter 17
Kissing Cousins

How can we bless or minister to people if we shut them out and cut them off?

—Larry Ferguson

Someone once said that Gospel and country music are kissing cousins. I think this is a fair assessment. Most country singers began their singing or musical careers in church and many Gospel singers learned to play their instruments, or found inspiration, from listening to the Grand Ole Opry. It's upsetting to me that while the Country Music industry fully welcomes Gospel artists, many in the Gospel industry snub or label the Country Music people as a *bunch of sinners*.

The attitude of some in the church world is that if an artist performs songs that are not Gospel, he or she is not living right. In many ways, this statement is hypocritical. Look at it this way: would you call an architect a sinner if he or she designs buildings other than churches? No, they are simply human beings working for a living. The same should apply with country singers.

A friend once argued with me about this point. "Music is different," he said, "because it affects the mind and lifestyle."

Yes, music can set the mood for many things but it is up to us as individuals how to discern what we should or should not allow on our stereo systems. How can we bless or minister to people if we shut them out and cut them off? Jesus was the best example of this; He went where believers wouldn't go and He talked with those outside the faith. The people society shunned, Jesus sought and befriended.

Many country artists have a true relationship with Christ or have high moral standards. One artist that comes to mind is Skeeter Davis. Skeeter loved God more than the air she breathed. Officials once suspended her from the Grand Ole Opry for using its airwaves to rebuke the Nashville Police Department for arresting street evangelists. Skeeter often used her Opry slot to sing a Gospel song instead of one of her hits. Many times, you could hear Skeeter singing one of Dottie's classics like *If That Isn't Love* or *I Go to the Rock* on the Grand Ole Opry.

Many times when Dottie performed in Nashville, an inconspicuous

Skeeter Davis sat in the back row enjoying every minute of the evening. Skeeter never wanted recognition and never wanted to go backstage before or after the program. That's just the way she was.

Skeeter caught Dottie on a TBN appearance and called my office. She told me how she enjoyed watching Dottie on the program and that she couldn't believe how great Dottie looked and how much stronger she had gotten. She went on to explain how she kept up with Dottie's career and she considered Dottie one of her heroes. She also mentioned how overseas promoters would tell her she couldn't preach or talk about the Lord, but during those concerts she would always sing *If That Isn't Love* and the promoters never questioned its lyrics.

Ricky Skaggs, his wife, Sharon White, and their singing group The Whites have been vocal about their faith. The Whites have recorded many of Dottie's songs and Ricky has always spoken highly of her. We had the pleasure of attending Ricky's induction into the Kentucky Music Hall of Fame and first he thanked Jesus Christ for his gifts during his acceptance. Both Ricky and The Whites were a part of a tribute special that TBN produced in honor of Dottie's music.

Emmylou Harris poses with Christian at a movie premier

We have crossed paths with many country singers over the years. In 2002, Dottie performed with Stella Parton and Marty Raybon at the Christian Country Music Awards. Little did she know,

Judy and Larry with Tanya Tucker

Crystal Gayle was going to present her with the Living Legend Award! Sitting in the audience until her number, Dottie felt the call of nature and needed to visit the little girl's room. As I took her backstage, Hank Williams Jr. had just finished his performance and security was clearing the way for him to get through the crowded hall.

"Everyone back up, please," the security officer announced. "Hank Williams Junior is coming through; step against the wall, please!"

We were halfway through the hallway (filled with other country and Gospel artists) when Dottie and I started to step back as the security officer had directed. However, when the officer saw Dottie Rambo stepping aside for Hank, he quickly changed his tune. "Everyone back up, Dottie Rambo is coming through," he said. "Hank, please scoot to the wall and allow Ms. Dottie to pass."

Hank graciously stepped against the wall. This embarrassed us that security would make Hank stand aside for Dottie to pass. However, it didn't bother Hank at all: he leaned over and placed a huge kiss on Dottie's cheek. That is a true Southern gentlemen.

Stella Parton is another dear friend. Stella started out in Gospel music with her own group *Stella Parton and the Gospel Carrolls*. Around that time, she recorded one of Dottie's songs (*Looks like Everybody's Got a Kingdom*) for

The incredible Stella Parton

a project never released (but I pray it will be someday). Stella has had great success in country music and even in theater. She has offered many kind words about Dottie in interviews and specials and we have had the pleasure of occasionally working with her on TBN as well. What has impressed me most about Stella is her sincerity. She doesn't just talk the talk—she lives and walks it.

Stella and I often bump into each other at the post office and she never lets me leave without a hug. Stella has always been genuinely kind to me...and *NOT* because I am Dottie's manager. This means a lot to me because many people in the business, or even so-called friends, will ignore

Larry Ferguson (the person) to talk with Larry Ferguson (Dottie Rambo's manager). Don't get me wrong, I love that people ask about Dottie, but at the same time, it's comforting when someone like Stella recognizes me as a person as well.

After the birth of my youngest son, Pierce, Stella sent a baby gift for him. It meant so much to us that Stella was kind enough to think of our newborn with all the comings and goings life brings. I'm not exactly sure how she knew about his birth, unless she read it in some of the Gospel trades, but we will never forget her generosity.

Visiting with Ralph Emery

Stella is not afraid to be bold either. My oldest son, Christian, wanted to go to the post office with me to get Dottie's fan mail. As I got Christian out of the car, Stella pulled in beside me. When Christian found out who Stella was, he started saying, "Will you tell Dolly hi for me? Tell Dolly I drew a picture for her!" I have to admit, this embarrassed me so I tried to keep him quiet.

"Stop that!" Stella said to me in a firm tone. "You are going to give that boy low self-esteem. You let him talk."

I quickly reminded myself Christian was just a five-year-old boy, and also realized Stella was secure in her skin, which made me love and respect her even more.

Another country friendship I have witnessed in Dottie's life has been with Marty Stuart. Marty wrote about Dottie in his book *Pilgrims, Sinners, Saints,*

Lulu Roman

and Prophets, which was a compilation of photos and thoughts about his musical influences. In his book, he recognizes Dottie as the most gifted songwriter he has known and said, "Her songs are a wide-open path to her spirit. And looking into her spirit is like staring into the sun. It's almost more than the eye can bear." I couldn't agree more.

During a local concert in Nashville, a knock came to the dressing room door and in walked an unannounced but welcomed Marty Stuart. He hugged, kissed, gushed and bragged on Dottie before the show. He also shared how he took a trip to the lake to be with the Lord and spent his time listening to Dottie's music and eating watermelon.

Marty turned to Dottie and said, "When are we going to write that song together, beautiful?"

"I don't know," Dottie replied. "When are we?"

"Well, you better get on it," Marty said with a laugh, "because I can outwait you if you let me."

Country artist and friend, Marty Stuart

On one of the occasions Dottie was in the hospital, a call came to the room and on the line was good ole Marty. He held true to the scripture: *A friend loveth at all times.*

Chapter 18
Miracles and More

Larry Ferguson loves his work! His loyalty and commitment to Dottie is evident by his tireless efforts on her behalf and that is a rare quality I admire a great deal.

—Ann Downing

My first flight with Dottie Rambo was one that will remain in my mind forever. Televangelist Benny Hinn invited Dottie to be a guest on his weekly television program, *This Is Your Day,* filmed in Orange County, California. Our flight was just after the tragedy of September 11, 2001. Security was at its highest level and everything going through an airport was scrutinized. Boy, was I in for a wake-up call!

For starters, we had too many bags to check in at the luggage counter. Being the cheapskate that I am, I told the attendant at check-in that I would take one of the bags (which happened to be Dottie's) as a carry-on. The attendant quickly told me that if I were to take the bag as my carry-on, I would need to be the owner of the bag and know exactly what was in it. Well, as I mentioned, this was Dottie's bag but I, being her travel companion, didn't think this rule would apply to our situation. So I assured the attendant the bag was mine (after all it was a bag within my party). Big mistake!

I quickly made my way down to the security checkpoint as I needed to hurry back to Dottie, who had an escort to the waiting area for the flight. While going through the checkpoint, every alarm imaginable went off! The security officer looked at me with interest.

"Is this your bag?" she asked with a raised eyebrow.

I nodded, assuring her it was. She took a peek inside the bag and asked, "Are you *sure* this is your bag?" she asked while rifling through its contents. "You do know you cannot carry a bag onboard unless it belongs to you and you know everything inside it, right?"

I again assured her with another nod. Perspiration beaded my forehead when she told me she would have to perform a bag search.

She motioned for a male security officer to join her and together they started their search. The first items removed were a few of Dottie's night-

*With Benny Hinn on the set of
"This Is Your Day"*

gowns and a huge make-up organizer. The officers looked at me with greater interest as they removed more nail polish, women's clothes and other female things. The male officer steals a glance at the female officer before turning his attention to me. "So," he said with a mocking tone, "are you going to do a show?"

As if having a hotflash, my cheeks and neck grew warm as I stood there wishing I had the ability to disappear into thin air. "No!" I said, trying to preserve some form of dignity. "But it's on its way to someone who is." Finally, after the officers found a pair of sewing scissors, they allowed me to continue.

We made it to Orange County safely and arrived at Benny Hinn's studios the next morning. As we waited in the greenroom, Pastor Benny came by to visit with Dottie. He also extended a warm welcome to me, which I didn't expect. I found him to be a calm and personable man. As he stood to walk out of the room, he turned back to me and said. "God chose you to take care of this woman. Watch over her!" Those words may be simple, but coming from Benny Hinn it was almost a decree.

Over the years Benny Hinn has become the victim of many jokes, accusations and negative press. Many skeptics doubt the healings in his services and have gone so far as even doubting his sincerity. Never have I met a man who was more sincere about his calling than Benny Hinn. Every service Dottie has taken part in has been anointed and you could feel the presence of God. Mr. Hinn will be the first to tell you that he doesn't heal anyone and that healing comes from Jesus Christ. I have much respect for this man of God.

A year or so down the road, the Benny Hinn Crusade came to my hometown of Louisville, Kentucky. The organizers invited Dottie to serve as a musical guest for all the services of the crusade. It was almost angelic hearing the unified voices of 15,000 people singing *Alleluia*. People from all walks of life came forward to be saved.

What you don't see on the television crusades are the thousands that come forward earlier in the service for salvation and how Benny explains to the attendees that without a spiritual new birth the physical healing is meaningless.

In attendance at the crusade was Donna Summer, who became a Christian in the eighties and now has a ministry of her own. Pastor Hinn unexpectedly called Donna to the stage and asked her to sing. Donna chose the old hymn *His Eye Is on the Sparrow* and breathed new life into the classic.

Before the final service ended, Benny called for everyone on the stage to come forward for prayer. Somehow I didn't hear him say this, but I did notice people were going through the prayer line onstage.

As some of the prayer assistants came to take Dottie for prayer, my mind and eyes were focused on her every move. You see, unlike the Benny Hinn Crusades, we have been to many church services where a non-anointed pastor would hurt Dottie while trying to pray for her. So as a rule, whenever anyone takes Dottie for prayer I watch like a hawk to make sure it is a moving of the Holy Spirit and not just a spectacle.

With my eyes glued to Dottie, I had missed the fact that even I should have gone forward for prayer as the whole stage was directed to do so. I felt a gentle touch on my arm as someone was trying to get my attention. I ignored the touch, keeping my eyes on Dottie. After another gentle touch on my arm I responded without turning to see who was trying to get my attention.

"Don't you want to go up to be prayed for?" a woman's voice asked.

"No," I said without taking my eyes off Dottie. "I'm fine, thank you."

"Are you sure you don't want to go up to be prayed for?" the calming voice asked again.

"No, I'm ok."

"It's just prayer," she said. "It won't hurt."

I turned around and realized the sweet voice belonged to Donna Summer. Now imagine how foolish I felt. I wanted to laugh, cry and hide all at the same time for not realizing I was the only one onstage not wanting to be prayed for, and here this sweet woman is trying to counsel me.

"I'm sorry," I said with a stutter. "I know it doesn't hurt, I do believe in what is happening and I'm already a Christian." I thought again how the gift of disappearing would come in especially handy at times like this. "I am Dottie Rambo's manager," I blurted out, "and I don't want to leave her out of my sight in case someone became unknowingly too rough with her."

Donna gave me a big smile and said she understood. That didn't help my embarrassment, though. I left that crusade with great respect for Donna, as not too many people of her stature would take the time to worry about someone's soul or spiritual well-being. She may not remember this incident but I will never forget her thoughtfulness.

Before the night of the final service I witnessed something that had a lasting impact on my life.

Meeting Donna Summer for the first time

A beautiful African-American family had somehow made it past Benny Hinn's security team and came onstage after the crusade had ended. They made their way to where we were sitting and asked Dottie for an autograph. What caught my eye more than anything was the son. His legs were mangled, pointing sideways and twisted. I remember thinking how awful this child's life must be. None of them even mentioned his impairment, and the boy was all smiles and happy that he could get an autograph.

The next night, after Benny prayed for the sick, this same family was in the prayer line to come onstage and tell of their miracle. I spotted them and wondered what their miracle would be. My mind thought that maybe their mom just wanted to be on TV or get another autograph. Before I knew it, I saw the boy's legs. They were normal, straight and he was standing as strong as any child without a physical handicap. He was healed, and whether anyone else in that arena believed it, I knew God worked a miracle as this boy walked across the stage.

After getting Dottie back to the hotel room, she and I were on such a spiritual high that we hated to see the crusade end! Dottie eventually retired for the evening and Judy and I went to a nearby restaurant. As we enjoyed our late-night supper, a woman who had attended the crusade approached us.

I wanted to let you know that I saw you at the Benny Hinn crusade helping Dottie Rambo," she said.

"Yes, that was me," I said. "Wasn't the service wonderful?"

"Well, not really," she said. "I don't get into all that crazy mess. I came to hear Dottie sing and I was turned off by all that silly stuff. You know them people weren't healed."

With the most assured look I could give her, I said, "Lady, there was enough faith from praying Christians in that auditorium that we could have stopped a war through prayer. It's our faith and the power of prayer that bring miracles and I don't think there is anything silly about Christians praying and believing together."

The woman apologized and said, "I guess you're right. I never thought about that before."

What a combination: Dottie, Christian and a Harley!

Chapter 19
Vince Gill and Amy Grant

If Dottie has an Aaron or a Hur in her life, it is Larry Ferguson.

—Kenny Bishop

Vince Gill and Amy Grant are two names most music lovers easily recognize. Vince's career in Country Music bridges the gap between youth and traditional fans alike. Amy Grant is a female pioneer of the Contemporary Gospel music movement. No matter how you look at it, they are celebrities. Their marriage brought another welcome bridge between Gospel and country music artists.

During Gospel Music Week of 2004, ASCAP held a special reception for Dottie in honor of the release of Bill Gaither's *Dottie Rambo with Homecoming Friends* video. An elite group of publishers, Music Row executives and Christian management heads were celebrating this release with Dottie and Bill.

One of the executives present was Chaz Corzine, who is one of the nicest men in Christian music. Chaz loves the heritage of Gospel music and Dottie is

Vince Gill

Amy Grant with daughter, Corrina Grant Gill, visit with Larry and Dottie

one of his favorites. While at the party, Chaz received a call from Amy Grant. During the conversation, he mentioned he was at a reception for Dottie and Amy asked him to invite us to her home for a cookout.

As we pulled up to Amy's beautiful Southern mansion in the middle of the elite Belle Meade section of Nashville, I never dreamed how down-to-earth these two intriguing people would be. As Chaz led us to the backyard, I saw many contemporary Christian stars like Bart Millard of Mercy Me playing volleyball. Within a moment, Vince Gill extended his hand to greet us. He took the reins as host—and an excellent host he was. I still can't believe Vince Gill was serving Diet Cokes to me during the whole cookout.

Dottie and Vince chatted for a while, and I remember Dottie asking who he thought was the best mandolin player in town and Vince saying Buck White of the Whites trio was one of his favorites. Dottie bragged on the beautiful job Vince and Tim Surrett did on her tune *Tears Will Never Stain The Streets Of That City*.

It didn't take long before Amy would take over as Dottie's conversation partner, and Vince would become my chatting partner. I found him to be such a down-to-earth person with a heart to be the best father, husband and all-out incredible person he could be.

One of the funnier moments came when Amy's teenage daughter begged her mother to allow her to get a piercing. Amy sternly told her daughter no, but the girl continued begging. "If your dad says OK then we will discuss it later," Amy said, referring to her first husband, Gary Chapman. Gary was in Dottie's band for years before marrying Amy and becoming famous in his own right.

A sweet but persistent daughter continued with her pleading when Amy realized she had an ace in the hole. "Honey, I need to introduce you to someone special," she said to her daughter. "This woman has been a major influence on your father's life and his writing."

"Oh honey, I've not seen you since you were just a little bitty thing," Dottie said to the girl.

"Honey," Amy said to her daughter. "I want you to ask Ms. Dottie if she thinks you should have this piercing." I'm sure Amy knew what Dottie's thoughts would be before she ever told her daughter to ask.

"No honey," Dottie said. "I don't think you should. You are much too pretty of a girl to do this to your body."

"Ok, now go call your daddy and you tell him that Dottie Rambo said you shouldn't get the piercing," Amy said with a victorious smile. "And *then* if he says you can have it, I'll even pay for it!"

Larry, Lori Bakker and Dottie

Chapter 20
Bill Anderson Visits with the Legends

I don't think the Devil wanted us to do this program
but we pulled it off!

—Bill Anderson

Good ole "Whispering" Bill Anderson is widely known for his *Po Folks* restaurants and legendary Grand Ole Opry status, but he also wears many hats in the industry. He has worked as a game-show host, a widely successful recording artist and one of country music's leading songwriters.

After learning Bill hosted the satellite radio program, *Bill Anderson Visits with the Legends,* I approached him about having Dottie on his show. Although we hadn't worked much with Bill, we had crossed paths on many occasions. Bill, of course, loved Dottie and her writing—and the feeling was mutual. The idea was one Bill quickly started to work on, and Dottie became the first Gospel legend to appear on the program.

Despite the excitement from everyone involved, the interview almost didn't happen. After scheduling the first session, Bill fell victim to the flu that invaded Nashville.

After rescheduling the date for a later taping, Dottie broke her femur during an accident in her home. After breaking the thickest bone in her body and enduring the surgery to repair it, Dottie spent several weeks in a physical therapy rehabilitation center. To pull the interview off, Bill decided to interview Dottie at the rehabilitation center.

The morning Bill was to set up shop, his producer's husband visited the emergency room after falling ill with a major health problem.

Determined to get the interview, Bill decided to do the show with only the folks in his tech crew.

"Well, Dottie," Bill said, walking into the room, "I don't think the Devil wanted us to do this program but we pulled it off!"

For well over an hour, Bill and Dottie discussed the highs and lows of her career and discovered they had much in common as well. Both were songwriters, both were inductees into several Halls Of Fame, both had endured the pain of divorce, and the list would multiply with each word of conversation between them.

Anderson is one of the great conversationalists of our time. His soothing voice has a welcoming quality and his preparation is as good as any entertainment reporter. Watching him interview Dottie made me wonder why he hadn't added television talk show host to his list of accomplishments.

When the interview was complete, we talked Bill into signing Dottie's cast, and took several photos to remember the occasion. This story should serve as proof that both Dottie and "Whispering Bill" will go to great lengths to make sure the public gets the program it deserves.

Bill Anderson signing Dottie's cast

Chapter 21
Hollywood and Tammy Faye

The paparazzi pounced on Britney's vehicle like a pack of wild animals after prey. We stood, watching wide-eyed and bewildered.

—Larry Ferguson

While traveling from coast-to-coast, I have learned to appreciate the landscapes and ambience of each state and city. I am amazed at the cultural diversity within the borders of our beautiful country. And traveling through these various states and cities, I have come to realize God has the eye of an artist, and that His creations are breathtaking. I am convinced that if the earth is God's canvas, His most beautiful work of art is California.

My few visits to the Golden State were those of hectic schedules and heavy workloads. We simply had no leisure time for shopping, fine dining or general sightseeing. However, on one particular tour with Dottie, I was able to enjoy some wonderful sites with my wife, Judy, who was with child at the time, and our four-year old son, Christian.

Don't get me wrong, we worked in several cities during this trip: Bakersfield, Van Nuys, Sacramento, Los Angeles and West Hollywood, where a pastor booked Dottie for a church service with Tammy Faye (Bakker) Messner.

That particular venue was far different from our typical concert crowd. While Dottie attracts all age groups, most of the crowd in the West Hollywood church consisted of people under thirty. Focusing on the homeless, prostitutes, drug addicts and dealers, this church was a new work but growing steadily.

As a blessing to Dottie and my family, the church asked that when we came for the concert we plan a mini-tour and allow their ministry to treat us to a working vacation. Therefore, we called Beverly Hills home for two weeks.

Each morning after breakfast, Judy, Christian, and I would leave the Beverly Hilton Hotel and walk the beautiful streets of Beverly Hills. Dottie had lived there during the 1980's so she was able to tell us where the best shops and must-see places were.

Larry, Tammy Faye and Judy

On one particular stroll, we found a crowd of photographers swarming an office building and moved closer to find out what was going on. One photographer told us pop star Britney Spears was inside getting her teeth cleaned at the dentist and was on her way out. I wasn't too familiar with Spears and did not care to see her make her getaway, but Christian insisted we wait until the pop princess came out.

A few minutes later, Britney and her fiancé (now husband), Kevin Federline, jumped into an automobile with what seemed like a dozen entourage members. The photographers ran in every direction as the automobile merged into congested traffic. Some of these photographers ran on foot and some jumped into cars, ready for a high-speed chase.

The paparazzi pounced on Britney's vehicle like a pack of wild animals after prey. We stood, watching wide-eyed and bewildered. "Daddy, why did they chase her?" Christian asked. "Do you think she forgot to pay her bill?"

Dottie's friend, Jerry Ashmore, happened to be in Los Angeles during that time for a work-related convention. Jerry has followed Dottie all around the country since he was fifteen and is one of the nicest people you would ever dream of meeting. When Jerry found out the Dottie Rambo clan was in town, he hunted us down. Each night Jerry treated my family to various eateries and sight-seeing stops.

While living in Beverly Hills, Dottie occupied the former home of screen legend Jean Harlow before buying a ranch in Laguna Hills.

My curious nature wouldn't allow me to rest until I saw this historic home. Dottie couldn't remember the address but gave me some identifying details. She told me it had a U-shaped driveway and the entire backyard was a swimming pool. Jerry, being my partner in crime, decided he would help us find the house as he had the address in his Dottie Rambo keepsakes.

It was late at night when we approached the old house, but we weren't sure if this was the right place. I suggested we drive down the alley and see if we could see a swimming pool for a backyard. Jerry drove us through an alley and unfortunately, the owners had erected a privacy fence.

Jerry suggested I stand on the roof of his car and peek over the fence. Normally the voice of reason in my life, Judy laughed and encouraged me to do as Jerry said.

After climbing onto the top of Jerry's car…in the alley of this posh Beverly Hills neighborhood…I was still too short to see over the fence!

"Maybe if you jump up and down you can see over the fence," Jerry said, chuckling.

"If I do that I'll dent the roof of your car."

"Well, it's not my vehicle, it's a rental," he said, smiling. "And I bought the extra insurance, so go ahead."

I looked at my feet, then at the fence, and decided to do it! As soon as I made my first jump, Judy yelled, "Here come the cops!"

I literally jumped off the roof of the car and landed in the alley on my behind! Terrified of receiving a citation as a Peeping Tom, I scrambled into the car, where everyone laughed hysterically. Even Christian was having a laugh at dear ole dad.

Judy's cop warning may have been a joke, but it was a wake-up call for me to avoid anything that would make me fear the wrath of police authorities.

A few days later, someone else drove Dottie and me past the house so Dottie could see it once again for herself. "Let's pull in the drive and ask the people if they mind us taking a picture of the house," Dottie said.

Now keep in mind, Dottie is dressed like a movie star and sporting shades … and we just drove up in a beautiful Cadillac complete with our own driver. After giving the door a knock, we heard the voices of an elderly couple talking inside the house. "Don't open the door, Archie," the woman said. "They look mighty peculiar."

Dottie gave me a this-is-going-to-be-interesting look and leaned in toward the door. "Hello," she said as if speaking to someone with hearing problems. "My name is Dottie Rambo, and I used to live in this house; would it be OK for us to take a picture of it?"

"Absolutely not," the man said from behind the closed door. "I don't believe you lived here; now get out of here before I call the police."

"I'm sorry," Dottie said. "We didn't mean any harm."

As we walked away, I heard the woman say, "I'm glad they didn't try to rob us!"

I thought how fortunate I was that this couple didn't discover me on top of a car peering over their fence a few nights before. If they feared someone like Dottie Rambo would rob them, they would probably shoot a

Peeping Tom like me on the spot!

I was happy to see the church in West Hollywood heavily publicizing the Dottie Rambo/Tammy Faye event with billboards, posters, flyers, radio and television ads. Much energy centered on that night as it was the first appearance these women had made together since the days of the PTL Network.

Their friendship goes back further than working together on PTL. However, the network is where their relationship grew. Jim and Tammy not only pioneered the PTL network, but also did the same for CBN and TBN. Without question, this couple was the Adam and Eve of Christian televi-

Tammy Faye with Christian

sion … although both would end up sacrificing far more than just a rib.

Dottie helped raise funds for all three networks with her family trio. Christian television was in its infancy then and The Rambos were one of the first groups to embrace it. Many referred to Dottie's family trio as *The Bridge* as they were one of only a few groups involved with all three stations.

There are many variations of what brought PTL to its demise. I don't care to dwell on any of the accusations or stories as I refuse to take away from the good that took place through the network and the ministry of Jim and Tammy Bakker.

Up to that night in West Hollywood, many changes had taken place in both lives of these women, most of which happened in the public eye. Tammy and Dottie both suffered public divorces and both endured health struggles. In the early 1990's, Tammy would win a battle with colon cancer only for it to return in her lungs in 2004.

At the time of that service, the cancer attacking her body was inoperable. Where most people would have succumbed to self-pity and depression, Tammy Faye leaned on her faith stronger than ever. And because of it, millions heard the Gospel message on secular news channels each night as the coverage of her cancer made headlines. Going through regular chemotherapy treatments, Tammy intentionally took a break from her medical visits to minister with Dottie that night.

People lined up along the streets of Santa Monica Boulevard, hoping for good seats. An eclectic gathering of worshipers filled the sanctuary. Pastors, prostitutes, photojournalists—you name it and they were there. Two film crews were also filming specials on Tammy Faye. Scenes from the evening would eventually appear on *E! True Hollywood Story* and on the *Women's Entertainment Network*.

In a tiny greenroom backstage, Dottie and Tammy caught up on old times as they searched through their purses, showing off makeup supplies. Between reminiscing and candid girl talk, Dottie asked if Tammy had suffered any hair loss from her chemotherapy.

"No," Tammy said. "But God must have a sense of humor because *all* my eyelashes fell out!" Tammy laughed as she referred to her trademark lashes that had once been the topic of many late night talk shows.

God set a spiritual banquet that night and everyone in the building feasted on what His two servants brought to the table. Dottie sang from the depths of her heart, and Tammy shared from her personal tragedies, while delivering a message of hope. That message rang clear as she is a living testimony of God's grace.

These ladies are no stranger to the pulpit, nor are they conventional ministers. They presented a kinder yet uncompromising approach to the Gospel message that night. They knew what worship was. They also knew that even in California, where hype and abundance are plentiful, people still hungered for real messengers…with real lives…serving a real God.

Tammy led an altar call that welcomed thirteen souls to Christ. Without the temptation of gimmicks or prizes, these people came forward with the promise of knowing Jesus Christ on a personal level. At that moment, I believe that any spirit trying to come against Tammy Faye—be it cancer or vengeful tongues—stood back as the Holy Spirit worked through her.

God's Anointing filled this sanctuary, and being obedient to the Lord, Dottie felt an urgency to serve Tammy Faye communion. As she served the communal cup, she said, "Tammy, I'll stand behind you waving every flag you need for me to wave."

"I stand behind you too," Tammy replied in tears. "You know I do. I love you so much."

With the Spirit of God leading, Dottie laid her hands on Tammy Faye and prayed for healing from the disease invading her body—prayed that every day would be a new day for Tammy Faye, that the Lord would heal her lungs and that she would sing more powerfully than ever before.

"Oh, I knew I was going to leave here healed!" Tammy said.

When Tammy went back to her North Carolina home, she soon learned that her cancer was in remission and no longer needed chemotherapy. However, in April of 2005, she received word that cancer once again invaded her body. I know that God will heal her again, and although I don't understand why she has to endure this again, I know she will have a stronger ministry for it.

This lady could have coined the phrase, "Keep on keeping on," because that is exactly what she does. Despite abandonment, ridicule, and personal hardships, Tammy Faye Messner has never silenced her love for Christ. And she continues to use every opportunity to speak of Him.

Chapter 22
Life without the Chauffeur's Hat

Daddy, when I become a singer, I want you to be my manager.

—Christian Ferguson

Many people ask what I do with my *spare* time. Someone asked me this once at a concert and Dottie jokingly said, "What spare time?" There's a lot of truth in that statement. I take pride in what I do and feel blessed to be working with Dottie. My family is my priority next to God—and Dottie *is* family.

Even when we are not traveling, I see Dottie every day. I am a homebody and rarely get out socially as far as the industry goes. Invitations to parties and industry events are common, especially when I first came with Dottie but rarely have I taken people up on them. Not that I am a snob or too good to socialize, I'm just too much of a hermit. When I'm not working, I enjoy spending time with my wife and children.

I love Hollywood and all memorabilia associated with it. Photos of me with my favorite singers and Hollywood celebrities line the walls of my residential office. These are memories I cherish. My photographs and memorabilia are keepsakes and treasures I hold dear to my heart.

My collection includes many items including a pair of *Mae West's* earrings, the nurse outfit *Lily Tomlin* wore in the *Beverly Hillbillies* movie, a *Susan Lucci* dress from *All My Children*, and a pair of *Dolly Parton's* high-heeled shoes. Not to mention all my Dottie Rambo keepsakes!

Knowing my love for music and old Hollywood, my wife arranged a birthday trip for me to Austin, Texas, to see Carol

Hamming it up with Pierce and Christian

Larry poses with Susan Lucci

Channing star in her show *The First 80 Years Are the Hardest.* Judy not only treated me to the show, but also to dinner with Carol the next evening at the home of Doctors Ken and Joanne Hunter. On the way to the Hunter's home, Carol shared how excited she was that I was from Nashville.

"Oh, I did a record there," she said. "You're probably too young to know who Webb Pierce is."

"Oh no," I said. "I know who he is."

"You do? What about Jimmy C. Newman?" She was even more delighted to learn that I knew who Jimmy C. Newman was. "I love Nashville," she said. "I once did a record with both Webb Pierce and Jimmy C. Newman. I also sang at their Grand Ole Opry. Is that still going on?"

"Yes, every weekend," I said, grinning. "And Jimmy C. Newman still sings on it about every weekend."

Talking with Carol Channing is like talking to a real-life angel—at least what I have always thought an angel would be like had I met one: fair-skinned, youthful and graceful all at the same time, displaying such a pure childlike innocence that I have never witnessed with anyone else. Don't get me wrong, I am not saying Carol Channing is an angel, but there's no doubt her talent came from the place where angels reside.

As the six of us dined, Carol—seated next to me—shared with us the story of how she and her husband, Harry Kullijian, wed. She explained they were childhood sweethearts and lost touch in their teenage years. However, a strange thing happened after Carol mentioned Harry in her autobiography, *Just Lucky I Guess.*

"I thought I had to write about my first love," she said. "And to be honest, I thought he was dead." A big smile stretched across her face as her eyes twinkled with mischief. "After all, he was older than me!" Laughter exploded as Carol's gaze scanned each person in the room.

A common friend reintroduced them, putting in motion a rekindling of their childhood romance. God couldn't have sent a better man for Carol

Carol Channing

than Harry. Within minutes of meeting him, I could see how much they loved each other. They were like two giddy school kids smitten with love for the first time. Their affection became the topic of conversation throughout the evening and Harry said, "I told Carol she hasn't seen anything yet; wait until you turn 90!"

As we dined and conversed, Carol would pat me on the back and announce to the others, "Isn't he such a good boy!" I couldn't help but blush; however, I enjoyed the attention paid by such a special woman.

Sharing a wonderful meal and spending time with Carol are memories no amount of money could equal. Later on that evening, as we sat in the living room area, a small chorus from the local high school entertained us. While listening to this private concert, Carol reached over and held my hand the entire time.

Another celebrity encounter came about when I, Chris Barnes and another friend, Chris Dossenbach, took a trip to New York. Before going on the trip, I felt like I was on the Bob Newhart Show. Remember what the character said? "Hello, my name's Larry. This is my brother, Daryl, and this is my *other* brother, Daryl." Insert Chris in the place of Daryl and you have the same effect—a*nd I guess we're only brothers in the Lord.*

I begged Judy to take the trip with us, but she prefers the Hamptons to the city and declined. So we (the guys) set out for the Big Apple. Our sole purpose for this trip was to see the insanely funny Joan Rivers. Joan is not only one of my favorite performers; she is one of Dottie's favorites as well. Any Dottie Rambo fan knows that after Dottie gets the audience on a roll of laughter, she usually follows up with the comment, "They call me the clean-mouthed Joan Rivers!" Dottie has always wanted to meet Joan too, but didn't get to go with us on this particular trip.

I have to admit, New York City can be intimidating. The roaring traffic, endless buildings and fast-paced society stand in stark contrast to life in Tennessee. With all that aside, New York can be alluring and eventful.

Joan was performing in a quaint place called the Cutting Room. Our table sat against the stage, leaving us an open target for the Comedy Queen. Joan asked me questions from the stage nearly the entire show, leading into her monologue and hilarious quips.

Backstage, she was the most wonderful and gracious person—a beautiful and petite woman who in most recent years has become the Queen of Hollywood's Red Carpet Events. For years, Mr. Blackwell was the *go-to* person when it came to fashion approval; however, Mr. Blackwell's pen cannot compare with the sharp and tasteful fashion assessments of Joan Rivers. Therefore, you can imagine what a compliment it was when Joan bragged on my outfit. Coming from anyone else, I would just assume it was a polite gesture, but when Joan comments on clothing, it is like winning an award!

Ms. Rivers recommended several Broadway shows for us to consider and talked with us for a long time. Not wanting to keep her, I began to dismiss my party, but Joan asked the boys and me to wait for just a moment. Joan, the gracious host that she is, gave each of us a beautiful red rose. I will never part with mine.

Chris Dossenbach, Larry, Joan Rivers and Chris Barnes

"Ah, you will look so cute carrying those roses around, if you go on the West Side," Joan teased.

Photography is another hobby of mine and has led to several celebrity meetings. I do some freelance photography for music magazines occasionally, and on assignment for a music publication once, I shot photos of Loretta Lynn onstage at the Grand Ole Opry. While there, I noticed

Yes, that's Anna Nicole Smith

Anna Nicole Smith walking in the building. I know you would never dream of reading her name in a book like this, but she was actually warm and friendly.

I firmly believe in treating everyone I meet in the same manner I want him or her to treat me. I also try directing my entire judgmental attitude toward myself. Therefore, I do not think meeting folks like Anna Nicole Smith is a shameful thing, and I proudly display our photo together! Now, would I recommend her for *Evangelist of the Year*? Absolutely not.

I've met many wonderful people from rockers like Bonnie Raitt, Jack White, and Carl Perkins to country music's George Jones, Emmylou Harris, and Brenda Lee—not to mention, great Hollywood personalities like Bob Hope, Delta Burke, Susan Lucci and countless others. No matter how I meet them I enjoy the memories. I think life is too short not to have a little fun.

My son Christian follows in his father's footsteps in many ways. Pierce may do so as well, he's too young to tell right now. Both boys love music and Christian loves people. I don't think he has ever met a stranger and rarely leaves the house without his CD and CD player.

Probably the greatest feeling in the world comes during the birth of your child. Until you have a child of your own, you can never fully experience the love that connects a parent and child.

When you come home from a hard day at work, nothing feels better than knowing you have a loving family waiting at home. I'm talking about a family who not only loves you, but also supports and believes in you. I have been fortunate to have that support. My wife and children keep my life as balanced as it can be, and each gives me a reason for waking up each morning.

As much as I have enjoyed meeting celebrities, traveling the country, meeting new and interesting people and all the memories these experiences bring, nothing compares to certain memories of my children: for instance, seeing my boys take their first steps, hearing their first word-crammed sentence, or celebrating their birthdays. But even more special is that God saw fit to give me such a great companion to love, cherish, celebrate and share the lives of these beautiful children.

Many times the spouse of a music professional goes unnoticed. Believe me, Judy's work, support and help never go unnoticed, and her faith in the life we made together makes the work I do that much easier.

As I mentioned before, when Christian was just an infant, Dottie told us that in the Spirit, she saw him with a microphone in front of thousands. He tells me his dream is to be a singer working in movies. I'm sure sharing a song onstage with GranDot only adds fuel to his enthusiastic flame.

Emmylou Harris

One quiet day at home, Christian summed up what our future held. "Daddy, when I become a singer, I want you to be my manager." The serious look on his face was as cute as could be. "You can take me out to my concerts when you are not taking GranDot to hers!"

"Ah, good idea," I said, doing my best to hold back a toothy grin.

"We can have Pierce be one of my singers, too," he added.

"Well, what about Mama?" I asked. "We can't leave her out."

"Oh," he said with a contemplative look. "Well, she can sell my T-shirts and CDs!"

If we could see life through a child's eyes, it wouldn't be so complicated. Through the pain, joy, tears, laughter and adventures, God has been

Larry's secret ambition: to be the American Idol

with us all the way. I have wondered so many times why God has allowed Dottie to walk through the pain she has had to endure. Just as often, I have wondered why Satan comes against her the way he does.

Lucifer, the fallen angel we now refer to as Satan, once led the music in Heaven and was a beautiful angel with a God-given gift. Although favored by God, Satan became jealous and wanted to be God. From his jealousy and greed came his expulsion from Heaven. I wonder if the reason he attacks our little Dottie so much is that she's taken on the job he once had, and can never get back?

A happy family: Christian, Pierce, Larry and Judy

Chapter 23
Q & A

Through e-mail, fan letters or just meeting people out and about, you would be amazed at the questions I get about Dottie. Some are comical and some are just basic questions that only a fan would want to know. I have listed and answered some of the most common questions so you can learn more about Dottie, get a good laugh or just satisfy your nosey itch!

Q: Does Dottie wear a wig?

A: *No, that's all her hair.*

GranDot, Pierce, Larry and Christian

Q: Does Dottie take a makeup artist and hair stylist with her on the road?

A: *Nope, she does it all herself. Pretty good, huh?*

Q: Are you Dottie's son?

A: *We've adopted each other! But naturally Dottie only has one daughter, Reba Rambo McGuire.*

Q: Are you married to Dottie?

A: *This comes up a lot. Now, this has to be one of the craziest questions I get. But the answer is No. Dottie is like a mother to me. Dottie usually makes it a point to mention that I have a great wife and two beautiful children when she talks about me, so people don't get the wrong idea.*

Q: Is Dottie dating anyone since she is single?

A: *Nope, she said she would need a registered letter from Jesus to know for sure who the right man was for her. Therefore, she just keeps herself married to her ministry.*

Q: Were Vestal Goodman and Dottie sisters?

A: *No, only in the spiritual sense. They did call each other Big Sis and Little Sis. Guess who was the Little Sis?*

Q: What are Dottie's favorite movies?

A: *I'm not sure what her favorite movies are, but I do know she collects Bette Davis movies and loves her! The Lethal Weapon series is one of her favorites (can you imagine that?) and anything to do with court or law. She seems to love court-room dramas and mysteries, too. To take the question further, she detests vampires and horror movies.*

Q: Does Dottie have a favorite TV show?

A: *She loves Dr. Phil, and all the judge shows, like Divorce Court and Texas Law. She also loves Court TV and A&E. She of course watches countless preaching and ministry-oriented shows, and watches CMT and GAC channels often.*

Q: Does Dottie buy her clothes off the rack at stores? How does she get her stage clothes?

A: *She normally doesn't buy at the stores as she tries to be unusual and creative. If she were to buy clothing from a retail store, she redesigns it, adding stones, changing lengths and on and on until the outfit doesn't look at all the way it started. She is a great seamstress and designer in her own right. She has made many of her stage outfits herself—or if she did not make them herself, she designed them. Many of her beaded dresses have been made or worked on by Houri in Nashville, a great dress designer and seamstress. Manuel, the famed Country music designer for the stars, has also designed for her in the past.*

Q: Does Dottie have a favorite songwriter?

A: *She loves the writings of Fanny Crosby.*

Q: Does she have a favorite Southern Gospel group?

A: *She loves many, but in the glory days her favorite was the Sons of Song; and of the current groups, The Isaacs are one of her favorites.*

Q: Why isn't Dottie on all the Gaither videos?

A: *In the early days of the Gaither videos, Dottie wasn't able to attend all the video shoots as she was still going through quite a bit with her health. Bill extends invitations to those he would like to have and those that will work on each special. Dottie normally comes if invited. Bill did dedicate an entire video to Dottie's songs as a tribute to her. The project is entitled "Dottie Rambo with Homecoming Friends."*

Q: Which Gaither videos does Dottie appear on?

A: *Reunion, Moments to Remember, I'll Fly Away, Build a Bridge* and *Dottie Rambo with Homecoming Friends* as of 2005.

Q: What is Dottie's age?

A: *She'd kill me if I told ya'! So don't ask her either!*

Dolly Parton and the Dottie Rambo gang

Accepting CCMA awards

Judy and Dottie

Larry and Jonathan Martin

Pierce says his first words on stage, sort of

The legendary Hovie Lister

Larry, Sue Dodge and Judy

Shirley Caesar

Dottie, Eva Mae LeFevre and Larry

Terry McMillan, David Ponder, Dottie, Mark Lowry, Michael Sykes, Mr. and Mrs. Michael English and Larry at the recording studio

Amy Lambert Templeton, Pierce and Dottie

Rebecca Isaacs Bowman, Dottie, Sonya Isaacs and Larry

Larry's dear friend and prayer partner, Dorothy Jo Owens

Larry and Dottie with Michael English

Heading to a concert appearance

Larry and Dottie with Michael Langston

Afterword

Larry is a wonderful man that I'm proud to call a friend. I am very honored to be included in his book, *Driving Ms. Dottie* (I, too, love Ms. Dottie!). He has done a wonderful job and I'm sure you readers will enjoy it.

Musically Yours,
Dolly Parton

* * *

Larry Ferguson fell into our lives like a penny from Heaven. I have seldom met anyone with whom I was more impressed; he is a true gift to everyone whose lives he touches. It is rare today to find someone with his innocence, sincerity and sweetness. It is with great pleasure that I laud his wonderful new book—*I am proud to call him a good friend to me and my family.*

Lily Tomlin

P.S. — I wouldn't mind having my own Larry Ferguson!

* * *

It is so very marvelous the way God puts people in our lives that truly make a difference for us. God blessed my dear friend, Dottie Rambo, by putting Larry Ferguson into her life. His energy, talent and heart bless us all.

Barbara Mandrell

* * *

Larry Ferguson is a true family man—with a heart for his choice of ministry, making sure Dottie Rambo keeps blessing us with her personal appearances and her priceless songs. All of humanity is indebted to this kind and meticulous young man.

Lou Wills Hildreth

* * *

I've enjoyed knowing Larry for a long time. Watching him at work as he assists one of Gospel music's great treasures has been an inspiration to me on more than a few occasions. If Dottie has an Aaron or a Hur in her life, it is Larry Ferguson.

Kenny Bishop

* * *

What an awesome thing it is to see someone dedicate their life, mostly behind the scene, to keep this great ministry going. Dottie Rambo is my hero and I am very grateful to Larry Ferguson for what he is doing for my friend, His reward will be great.

God Bless,
Gerald Crabb

* * *

"It doesn't take long to know a true Christian. When I met Larry I saw in him a servant and a very talented man. What a blessing he is to Dottie. I'm glad Larry is my friend and brother in the Lord."

Betty Jean Robinson

* * *

Larry Ferguson is a minister ... ministering with the utmost excellence and sensitivity. His service to Dottie Rambo is regarded by churches and ministries around the world as "Ministries At Its Best", enabling Dottie to minister at her best. As a minister of the Gospel, I speak for the body of Christ when I say "Thank You Larry Ferguson," you are a blessing to us all.

Jessy Dixon

* * *

One of the many wonderful spiritual gifts that St. Paul mentioned, is the "ministry of helps" (I Cor. 12:28). Surely, Larry Ferguson is one of the finest examples that I know of this gift. His dedication to the ministry of Dottie

Rambo is a divine gift of "helps".... helping to bring to all of us her gift of music.

Little Jan Buckner-Goff

* * *

I was honored to be asked to say something about Larry Ferguson. I have known Larry "In The Line Of Duty" or should I say on the job for a few years now. I have found him to be the utmost professional. Not only that, he is one of the kindest, sweetest and loyal individuals I know. God bless him in this new work. If it is like everything else he does it will be impeccable.

—Stella Parton

* * *

Larry Ferguson loves his work! His loyalty and commitment to Dottie is evident by his tireless efforts on her behalf, and that is a rare quality I admire a great deal!

— Ann Downing

* * *

I only had to be around Larry Ferguson for a few minutes before I knew that his heart was dedicated one hundred percent to Dottie Rambo and her music. You'll be as convinced as I as he shares his collection of meaningful and memorable moments from this Gospel legend's remarkable career. He's been there, and the pages of this book take you there as well. Hang on...it's quite a ride!

— Bill Anderson

* * *

Larry Ferguson has blessed the countless Dottie Rambo fans by taking us behind the scenes and allowing us to become acquainted with the gracious and warm-hearted person that she is. At the same time, he reveals his own dedication and passion for ministry through serving others. Behind those who are in the public limelight, there are faithful, unseen helpers upon whom they depend for effective ministry. This book illustrates the great principle that, just as each member of the physical body has its assigned purpose, God appoints us to various kinds of ministry to ensure that the body of Christ functions as a whole. I praise God that through Larry's ministry Dottie is free to fulfill her calling of blessing the world with anointed music.

— Donna Douglas

* * *

I hope everyone will love Larry Ferguson's collection of stories as much as I did. Both Dottie and Larry are lucky to have each other, and I am happy to be included in Driving Ms. Dottie. I hope everyone will read it from cover to cover.

— Tammy Faye

* * *

Jump in for a joyride as Larry Ferguson takes us on a journey of laughter and reflections in Driving Ms. Dottie—and best of all, everybody gets a window seat and Larry pays for the gas!!! *Bless his heart!*

—Aaron Wilburn

* * *

It was a great blessing working with you on the Dottie Rambo Tribute television production. Thank you for sharing your inspirational message of love, hope and optimism.

—Crystal Gayle

Thank You

Dottie Rambo — If I used a million words to tell you how much I love you that still wouldn't be sufficient. Thank you for being my spirit mother and the GranDot to my children. I'm thankful to God for the privilege to know you let alone work side by side with such a chosen vessel.

Dorothy Jo Owens — Had it not been for your encouragement, prayers, friendship and support I may never have been able to complete this project. Your prayers were felt the entire time during the writing of this manuscript. Thank you for being a prayer partner and dear friend.

Judy, Christian and Pierce Ferguson — Thank you so much for all the happiness you bring me. I love you unconditionally.

Jackie (MOM) Burgess — Thank you for believing in me more than I ever have in myself. Your protection and love have guided and shielded me through many storms and wrong turns.

Larry (DAD) Ferguson, Sr. — Thank you for instilling the seed of music deep within my soul. I only wish I had an ounce of the talent that you have. Thank you most of all for being proud of me and finally coming around to my music ... well sorta. HA.

Chris Barnes — One day you can write a book titled, "Driving the one who drives Ms. Dottie". Thank you for being the best friend a person could ask for. No matter what the task, or what I need to vent about, you are always there. I can't thank you enough.

Nick Burgess — Thank you for being the greatest stepfather a person could ever want!

Linda and Ed Howard — Thank you for bringing Judy in the world for me!

Mike and Jewell Collins, associates of Woodland Press — Thank you for all the work you put into making sure that *Driving Ms. Dottie* was a success. Most of all, thank you for allowing me to be me during our work together. Your concern, persistence and enthusiasm mean more to me than you will ever know. I also appreciate the encouragement of your wife, Jewell.

Keith and Cheryl Davis, of Woodland Press — Thank you for believing in *Driving*

Ms. Dottie and wanting to take a chance to work with a published novice like myself. Dottie Rambo fans all over the world now can thank you for letting them see an inside glimpse of our Queen.

Tim and Renee Fortune, of Woodland Press — It was great to meeet you at the Logan, WV concert. Thank you for the behind-the-scene contributions to this project.

Dolly Parton, Lily Tomlin, Barbara Mandrell, Lou Hildreth, Kenny Bishop, Gerald Crabb, Betty Jean Robinson, Jessy Dixon, Little Jan Buckner, Stella Parton, Crystal Gayle, Aaron Wilburn, Bill Anderson, Ann Downing, Donna Douglas, Tammy Faye and Claude Hopper — Thank you for taking time to make contributions to *Driving Ms. Dottie.*

18th Street Baptist Church and Randy and Loise Constant — You will always be my home church and pastors for life. I love you dearly.

Reba Rambo, Destiny and Israel McGuire — Thank you for sharing your Grandot with me and my family. Her gifts will now live on through your very being. One day your offspring's own seed will look back and see the impact your Grandot's bloodline has had on the music world.

All Dottie's fans — Thank you for loving and believing in Dottie.

All Dottie's friends and family — Thank you for accepting and welcoming me into your lives.

Pam and Claude Walls, Nancy Hartlage, Chris Dossenbach, Sheena Dawson, Emily Holleman, Dr. Jerry Horner, Javetta Saunders, Cornelia Hutto, Bette Tillman, Barry Drudge, Beckie Simmons Staff, Billy Jones, Olan Witt, Richard Tomlin and Michael Langston — Your friendship, prayers and contributions to my life will never go unnoticed or unappreciated. I am blessed having known all of you.

Justin McIntosh, LaDanny, Neese B, James Blackmon, Bob and Susan Minzak, and Trumps — Thank you for helping pull together the greatest photo session we could create.

Additional thanks: Front cover photography by Justin McIntosh. Dottie Rambo's make up by Ladanny. Larry Ferguson's make up by Nese B. Larry Ferguson's hair by James Blackmon, Bob and Susan Minzak. Non-cover photos courtesy of: Author's Collection, Mark Burgess, Chris Barnes and Cornelia Hutto. Additiional thanks: Estate of Bob and Susan Minzak and The Dottie Rambo Collection.